# Accounting for Biological Assets

This book explores accounting for biological assets under International Accounting Standard (IAS) 41 Agriculture, and explains the recent adjustments introduced by the International Accounting Standards Board (IASB) which allow firms to choose between cost or revaluation models concerning mature bearer plants.

Identifying the firm and country-level drivers that inform the disclosure and measurement practices of biological assets, this concise guide examines the value relevance of measuring those assets at fair value. It also analyses how firm and country-level drivers explain the differences in the disclosure level and practices used to measure biological assets under IAS 41. Finally, it evaluates whether there is a difference in the relevance of biological assets among the listed firms with high and low disclosure levels on biological assets.

Based on a major international study of a wide selection of firms and country-level drivers, this book is vital for standard setters, stakeholders, students, accountants and auditors who need to understand disclosure and measurement practices of biological assets under IAS 41.

**Rute Gonçalves** is Accounting Supervisor at Centrar, S.A. RAR Group, Portugal. She has previously taught at the University of Porto, Portugal.

**Patrícia Teixeira Lopes** is Associate Dean at Porto Business School, University of Porto, Portugal. She was a research member of INTACCT, a European project on the application of the IAS/IFRS in Member States of the European Union.

# Routledge Focus on Business and Management

The fields of business and management have grown exponentially as areas of research and education. This growth presents challenges for readers trying to keep up with the latest important insights. Routledge Focus on Business and Management presents small books on big topics and how they intersect with the world of business.

Individually, each title in the series provides coverage of a key academic topic, whilst collectively, the series forms a comprehensive collection across the business disciplines.

ISSN: 2475–6369

*For a complete list of titles in this series, please visit* www.routledge.com/business/series/FBM

**Auditing Teams: Dynamics and Efficiency**
*Mara Cameran, Angelo Ditillo and Angela Pettinicchio*

**The Reflective Entrepreneur**
*Dimo Dimov*

**The Spartan W@rker**
*Konstantinos Perrotis and Cary L. Cooper*

**Writing a Business Plan: A Practical Guide**
*Ignatius Ekanem*

**Manager vs. Leader: Untying the Gordian Knot**
*Robert M. Murphy and Kathleen M. Murphy*

**Accounting for Biological Assets**
*Rute Gonçalves and Patrícia Teixeira Lopes*

# Accounting for Biological Assets

Rute Gonçalves and
Patrícia Teixeira Lopes

Routledge
Taylor & Francis Group

LONDON AND NEW YORK

First published 2018
by Routledge
2 Park Square, Milton Park, Abingdon, Oxon OX14 4RN

and by Routledge
605 Third Avenue, New York, NY 10017

First issued in paperback 2021

*Routledge is an imprint of the Taylor & Francis Group, an informa business*

© 2018 Rute Gonçalves and Patrícia Teixeira Lopes

The right of Rute Gonçalves and Patrícia Teixeira Lopes to be identified as authors
of this work has been asserted by them in accordance with sections 77 and 78 of the
Copyright, Designs and Patents Act 1988.

All rights reserved. No part of this book may be reprinted or reproduced or utilised
in any form or by any electronic, mechanical, or other means, now known or
hereafter invented, including photocopying and recording, or in any information
storage or retrieval system, without permission in writing from the publishers.

*Trademark notice*: Product or corporate names may be trademarks or registered trademarks,
and are used only for identification and explanation without intent to infringe.

Publisher's Note
The publisher has gone to great lengths to ensure the quality of this reprint but points out
that some imperfections in the original copies may be apparent.

*British Library Cataloguing-in-Publication Data*
A catalogue record for this book is available from the British Library

*Library of Congress Cataloging-in-Publication Data*
A catalog record for this book has been requested

ISBN 13: 978-1-03-209622-3 (pbk)
ISBN 13: 978-0-815-37141-0 (hbk)

Typeset in Times New Roman
by Out of House Publishing

# Contents

# List of tables

# List of appendices

# List of annexes

# List of abbreviations

| | |
|---|---|
| AASB | Australian Accounting Standards Board |
| CFO | Chief Financial Officer |
| CPC | *Comitê de Pronunciamentos Contábeis* |
| FASB | Financial Accounting Standards Board |
| GAAP | Generally Accepted Accounting Principles |
| IAS | International Accounting Standard |
| IASB | International Accounting Standards Board |
| IASC | International Accounting Standards Committee |
| IFRS | International Financial Reporting Standards |
| OLS | Ordinary Least Squares |
| PwC | PricewaterhouseCoopers |
| R&D | Research and Development |
| SBF | *Société des Bourses Françaises* |

# 1 Overview

International Financial Reporting Standards (IFRS)[1] have been recognised as a set of high-quality accounting standards. Despite having
already been adopted by almost 140 countries and other jurisdictions,
there are firm and country-level differences that explain the existing gap
in the goal of standardisation of those standards. This book explores
this gap for biological assets under International Accounting Standard
(IAS) 41 Agriculture. IAS 41 has motivated intense debate on accounting for agricultural activity, mostly due to introducing major changes in
the measurement of biological assets. This book also explores the value
relevance of fair value in biological assets.

As a first step, the book describes IAS 41 and explains its recent
adjustments introduced by the International Accounting Standards
Board (IASB). Secondly, in order to provide a better understanding of
IAS 41 in listed firms, a topic that has received little academic attention,
this research introduces two main accounting issues, namely: 1) to present the state of the art, to identify the firm and country-level drivers
that explain disclosure and measurement practices of biological assets
and to discuss the disclosure index and 2) to examine the value relevance of measuring those assets at fair value.

After discussing these accounting issues, the book provides worldwide evidence by exploring a selection of listed firms that comply with
the criteria of having first adopted IFRS or equivalent standards before
2012. The following questions will be answered in this book. What is the
disclosure level on biological assets in listed firms under IAS 41? What
firm and country-level drivers explain the differences in the disclosure
level on biological assets among listed firms? What firm and country-
level drivers explain the differences in practices used to measure biological assets among listed firms? Is there a difference in the relevance of
biological assets between listed firms with high and low disclosure levels
on biological assets?

This book aims to help standard setters, firms' stakeholders, students, accountants and auditors to better understand disclosure and measurement practices of biological assets and their drivers. Additionally, it contributes to the increased awareness of the market valuation implications of IAS 41 and to identify new areas of research on the issue of accounting for biological assets.

## Note

1  International Financial Reporting Standards (hereafter IFRS) are standards issued by the International Accounting Standards Board (IASB). Regulation (EC) no. 1606/2002 requires that listed firms in the European Union (EU) prepare their consolidated financial statements under IFRS for years beginning on or after January 1 2005. IFRS include International Accounting Standards (hereafter IAS) and their interpretations adopted by IASB from its predecessor, the International Accounting Standards Committee (IASC).

# 2 International Accounting Standard 41 Agriculture

IAS 41 was originally issued in December 2000 and first applied to annual periods beginning on or after 1 January 2003. There are other IFRS that have made minor consequential amendments to IAS 41. They include IAS 1 Presentation of Financial Statements (as revised in December 2003 and in September 2007), IAS 2 Inventories (as revised in December 2003), Improvements to IFRS (issued in May 2008), IFRS 13 Fair Value Measurement (issued in May 2011), and amendments by Agriculture: Bearer Plants (Amendments to IAS 16 Property, Plant and Equipment and IAS 41, issued in January 2016).

## Overview

IAS 41 prescribes the accounting treatment for biological assets during the period of biological transformation and for the initial measurement of agricultural produce at the point of harvest. In addition, the standard prescribes financial statement presentation and disclosures related to agricultural activity.

As a basic rule, IAS 41 requires that biological assets shall be measured on initial recognition and at subsequent reporting dates at fair value less costs to sell, unless fair value cannot be reliably measured. This exception is only applied on initial recognition. Moreover, agricultural produce shall be measured at fair value less costs to sell at the point of harvest.

This standard includes different methods in assessing the fair value estimate. Market value is preferred, if reliable. When market-based prices are not available, fair value is the present value of expected net cash flows from the asset, discounted at a current market rate (the discounted cash flows method). In some situations, historical cost is an allowed treatment.

## About IAS 41 and how it should be read

IAS 41 is set out in paragraphs 1–64. All of the paragraphs have equal authority but retain the IASC format of the standard when it was adopted by the IASB.

IAS 41 should be read in the context of its (a) objective and (b) basis for conclusions, (c) preface to IFRS and (d) conceptual framework for the financial reporting.

IAS 8 Accounting Policies, Changes in Accounting Estimates and Errors provides a basis for selecting and applying accounting policies in the absence of explicit guidance.

## Objective of IAS 41

The objective of IAS 41 is to prescribe the accounting treatment and disclosures related to agricultural activity.

## The scope of IAS 41 and its exemptions

**Scope.** IAS 41 shall be applied to biological assets (except for bearer plants), agricultural produce at the point of harvest and government grants related to biological assets [IAS 41.1].

**Exemptions from the scope.** IAS 41 does not apply to land related to agricultural activity (IAS 16 and IAS 40 Investment Property); bearer plants related to agricultural activity (IAS 16); government grants related to bearer plants (IAS 20 Accounting for Government Grants and Disclosure of Government Assistance); intangible assets related to agricultural activity (IAS 38 Intangible Assets); and right-of-use assets arising from a lease of land related to agricultural activity (IFRS 16 Leases) [IAS 41.2]. Furthermore, IAS 41 does not apply to agricultural produce after the point of harvest. Such produce will be inventory and treated by IAS 2 Inventories [IAS 41.3].

Examples of biological assets, agricultural produce, and products that are the result of processing after harvest [IAS 41.4] are presented in Table 2.1.

## Definitions

IAS 41 includes the following key terms:

a.  Agricultural activity: the management of the biological transformation and harvest of biological assets for sale, or for conversion into agricultural produce or into additional biological assets [IAS 41.5];

*Table 2.1.* Examples of biological assets, agricultural produce and products that are the result of processing after harvest

| Biological assets | Agricultural produce | Products that are the result of processing after harvest |
|---|---|---|
| Sheep | Wool | Yarn, carpet |
| Trees in a timber plantation | Felled trees | Logs, lumber |
| Dairy cattle | Milk | Cheese |
| Pigs | Carcass | Sausages, cured hams |
| Cotton plants | Harvested cotton | Thread, clothing |
| Sugarcane | Harvested cane | Sugar |
| Tobacco plants | Picked leaves | Cured tobacco |
| Tea bushes [1] | Picked leaves | Tea |
| Grape vines [1] | Picked grapes | Wine |
| Fruit trees | Picked fruit | Processed fruit |
| Oil palms [1] | Picked fruit | Palm oil |
| Rubber trees [1] | Harvested latex | Rubber products |

[1] These biological assets meet the definition of bearer plant; therefore, they are within the scope of IAS 16. Nonetheless, the corresponding produce growing, tea leaves, grapes, palm oil fruit and latex is within the scope of IAS 41.

b. Agricultural produce: the harvested produce of the entity's biological assets [IAS 41.5];

c. Bearer plant: a living plant that is used in the production or supply of agricultural produce which is expected to bear produce for more than one period and has a remote likelihood of being sold as agricultural produce, except for incidental scrap sales [IAS 41.5]; bearer plant excludes (a) plants cultivated to be harvested as agricultural produce (e.g. trees grown for use as lumber); (b) plants cultivated to produce agricultural produce when there is more than a remote likelihood that the entity will also harvest and sell the plant as agricultural produce, other than as incidental scrap sales (e.g. trees that are cultivated both for their fruit and their lumber); and (c) annual crops (e.g. maize and wheat) [IAS 41.5A];

d. Biological asset: a living animal or plant [IAS 41.5];

e. Biological transformation: the process of growth, degeneration, production and procreation that change the value or quantity of the biological asset [IAS 41.5];

f. Costs to sell: incremental costs directly attributable to the disposal of an asset (e.g. commissions to brokers and dealers, transfer taxes, duties and fees paid to regulatory agencies or commodity exchanges), excluding the cost of transporting the asset to market, finance costs and income taxes [IAS 41.5];

g. Harvest: the process of produce detaching from a biological asset or the cessation of its life [IAS 41.5];
h. Fair value: the price that would be received to sell an asset or paid to transfer a liability in an orderly transaction between market participants at the measurement date [IAS 41.8, amended by IFRS 13 Fair Value Measurement (2011)];
i. Consumable biological assets: the assets that are to be harvested as agricultural produce or sold as biological assets (e.g. livestock intended for the production of meat, livestock held for sale, fish in farms, crops such as maize and wheat, produce on a bearer plant, and trees being grown for lumber) [IAS 41.44];
j. Bearer biological assets: the assets that are not agricultural produce but, rather, are held to bear produce (e.g. livestock from which milk is produced and trees from which firewood is harvested while the tree remains) [IAS 41.44];
k. Mature biological assets: the assets that have attained harvestable specifications (for consumable biological assets) or are able to sustain regular harvests (for bearer biological assets) [IAS 41.45].

**Recognition and measurement**

Biological assets or agricultural produce are recognised when [IAS 41.10]:

a. The entity controls the asset as a result of past events;
b. It is probable that future economic benefits will flow to the entity; and
c. Fair value or cost of the asset can be reliably measured.

Biological assets shall be measured on initial recognition and at subsequent reporting dates at fair value less costs to sell, unless fair value cannot be reliably measured [IAS 41.12]. Agricultural produce shall be measured at fair value less costs to sell at the point of harvest. Such measurement is the cost at that date when applying IAS 2 Inventories [IAS 41.13]. Since harvested produce is a marketable commodity, there is no "measurement reliability" exception for agricultural produce.

In May 2011 (with an effective date in January 2013), the IASB issued IFRS 13 Fair Value Measurement which clarifies how to measure fair value and improves fair value disclosures. More precisely, IFRS 13 defines an active market and contains a three-level, fair value hierarchy for the inputs used in the valuation techniques used to measure fair value. This has an impact on how fair value of biological assets and agricultural produce at point of harvest is determined. IFRS 13 has guidelines for using valuation techniques to measure fair value. An entity shall apply those amendments in IAS 41 when it applies IFRS 13.

The fair value hierarchy (according to IFRS 13) consists of the following three levels:

a. Level 1 inputs are quoted prices in active markets for identical assets or liabilities that the entity can access at the measurement date. This level must be used without adjustment whenever available [IFRS 13:76];
b. Level 2 inputs are inputs not included within Level 1 that are observable for the asset or liability, either directly or indirectly [IFRS 13:81];
c. Level 3 inputs are unobservable inputs for the asset or liability, including the entity's own data, which are adjusted if necessary to reflect market participants' assumptions [IFRS 13:86].

Applying this hierarchy to biological assets, when an identical biological asset cannot be found in an active market or when no active market exists for the biological asset during its biological transformation, the entity would be required to measure fair value using a valuation technique that uses Level 2 and/or Level 3. Such a valuation technique might be a market approach (using prices for comparable biological assets or identical biological assets in an inactive market), an income approach (discounted cash flows) or a cost approach (current replacement cost).

The fair value measurement of a biological asset or agricultural produce may be facilitated by grouping biological assets or agricultural produce according to significant attributes; for example, by age or quality [IAS 41.15].

Cost may sometimes approximate fair value, when: (a) little biological transformation has taken place since initial cost incurrence (e.g. for seedlings planted immediately prior to the end of a reporting period or newly acquired livestock); or (b) the impact of the biological transformation on price is not expected to be material (e.g. for the initial growth in a 30-year pine plantation production cycle) [IAS 41.24].

## Recognition in profit or loss

The gain or loss on initial recognition of biological assets at fair value less costs to sell and changes in fair value less costs to sell of biological assets during a period are reported in profit or loss [IAS 41.26].

The gain or loss on initial recognition of agricultural produce at fair value less costs to sell shall be included in profit or loss for the period in which it arises [IAS 41.28].

## Inability to measure fair value reliably

IAS 41 includes a presumption that an entity can establish a fair value for biological assets [IAS 41. 30]. This presumption may be rebutted only on initial recognition and in singular conditions: a market-determined price is not available and the entity cannot assure a reliable estimate of fair value. In such circumstances, the entity recognises the biological assets at cost less depreciation and impairment.

Once the fair value of the biological asset becomes reliably measureable, the biological asset shall be measured at fair value less costs to sell. Once a non-current biological asset meets the criteria to be defined as held for sale, then it is presumed fair value can be measured reliably.

## Government grants

An unconditional government grant with respect to biological assets measured at fair value less costs to sell shall be recognised in profit or loss when, and only when, the government grant becomes available [IAS 41.34].

A conditional government grant, in which the grant requires an entity not to engage in specified agricultural activity, shall be recognised as income when, and only when, the conditions of the grant are met [IAS 41.35].

## Disclosure requirements of IAS 41

IAS 1 Presentation of Financial Statements requires that biological assets are presented separately on the face of the balance sheet [IAS 1.54(f)].

The disclosure required by IAS 41 comprises both financial and non-financial information that corresponds mainly to mandatory information (paragraphs [IAS 41.40–57]) and also to some recommended information (paragraphs [IAS 41.43] and [IAS 41.51]).

The financial statements shall disclose:

a.  Aggregate gain or loss arising during the period upon initial recognition of biological assets and agricultural produce [IAS 41.40];
b.  Change in fair value less costs to sell of biological assets during the period [IAS 41.40];

c. Narrative or quantified description of an entity's biological assets, by broad group [IAS 41.41; IAS 41.42];
d. Description of the nature of an entity's activities with each group of biological assets and description of non-financial measures or estimates of physical quantities (of assets on hand at the end of the period and of agricultural produce output during the period) [IAS 41.46];
e. Information about biological assets whose title is restricted or that are pledged as security [IAS 41.49];
f. Commitments for development or acquisition of biological assets [IAS 41.49];
g. Financial risk management strategies [IAS 41.49];
h. Reconciliation of changes in the carrying amount of biological assets, between the beginning and the end of the period, showing changes separately in value, purchases, sales, biological assets classified as held for sale, harvest, increases resulting from business combinations and foreign exchange differences [IAS 41.50].

Disclosure of a quantified description of each group of biological assets, distinguishing between consumable and bearer assets or between mature and immature assets, is encouraged but not required [IAS 41.43].

If fair value cannot be measured reliably, additional required disclosures include [IAS 41.54]:

a. Description of the assets;
b. An explanation of the circumstances;
c. If possible, a range within which fair value is highly likely to lie;
d. Depreciation method;
e. Useful lives or depreciation rates;
f. Gross carrying amount and the accumulated depreciation, at the beginning and end of the period.

If biological assets are measured at cost less any accumulated depreciation and any accumulated impairment losses, additional required disclosures include [IAS 41.55]:

a. Gain or loss recognised on disposal of biological assets;
b. Separate reconciliation of changes in the carrying amount of biological assets and additionally, the impairment losses, reversals of impairment losses and depreciation.

If the fair value of biological assets previously measured at cost now becomes available, certain additional disclosures are required [IAS 41.56]:

a.  Description of the biological assets;
b.  An explanation of the circumstances;
c.  The effect of the change.

Disclosure of the amount of change in fair value less costs to sell included in profit or loss due to physical changes and due to price changes, by group, is encouraged but not required [IAS 41.51].

Disclosures relating to government grants include the nature and extent of grants, unfulfilled conditions and significant decreases expected in the level of grants [IAS 41.57].

## Recent amendments

IASB has amended IAS 41 when it comes to bearer plants (prior to reaching maturity) and its measurement at accumulated cost, such as self-constructed items of property, plant and equipment. Entities are permitted to choose either the cost model or the revaluation model for mature bearer plants under IAS 16. Produce growing on bearer plants should be accounted for at fair value in accordance with IAS 41. These amendments are effective for annual periods beginning on or after

*Table 2.2.*  Historical development of IAS 41

| Date | Development | Comments |
| --- | --- | --- |
| December 1999 | Exposure Draft E65 Agriculture | Comment deadline 31 January 2000 |
| December 2000 | IAS 41 Agriculture issued | Operative for annual financial statements covering periods beginning on or after 1 January 2003 |
| 22 May 2008 | Amended by *Improvements to IFRSs* (discount rates) | Effective for annual periods beginning on or after 1 January 2009 |
| 30 June 2014 | Amended by *Agriculture: Bearer Plants (Amendments to IAS 16 and IAS 14)* | Effective for annual periods beginning on or after 1 January 2016 |

1 January 2016, with earlier application being permitted (European Commission, 2014).

In brief, three reasons have supported this change. Firstly, fair value measurement for bearer plants in the absence of the corresponding market is complex, costly and implies practical constraints. Moreover, changes in fair value less costs to sell are recognised in profit or loss and imply results volatility. Secondly, mature bearer plants are assumed to be manufacturing assets, since they are no longer undergoing significant biological transformation. Finally, the reported profit or loss is adjusted by financial users to eliminate effects of changes on fair valuation of bearer biological assets, because their focus is on the revenue from the produce growth of these assets. Overall, these adjustments are expected to reduce compliance costs, complexity and profit volatility for preparers, without a significant loss of information for users of their financial statements. IASB also provide relief from retrospective restatement by permitting an entity to use the fair value of an item of bearer plants as the deemed cost at the start of its earliest comparative period (European Commission, 2014).

Table 2.2 presents the historical development of IAS 41.

# 3 Accounting for biological assets
## Current debate

## State of the art: Disclosure and measurement

### Introduction

Bearing in mind a firm's financial position and performance, disclosure is a way of sharing economic, financial or non-financial, quantitative or qualitative information. Mandatory disclosure, at first sight, appears incongruent to analysis in terms of compliance. Furthermore, if firms are required to answer to specific information, ideally there would be no reason for differences to occur in disclosure reporting. Nonetheless, in accordance with Chavent et al. (2006), firms exercise some discretionary behaviour in financial reporting, where mandatory disclosures are concerned. Therefore, there is a close link with voluntary disclosure and both can be studied under the same theoretical framework. In the literature, the reason why firms voluntarily disclose information is related to several theories, namely: stakeholder theory, agency theory, signalling theory, legitimacy theory and political economy theory (Oliveira et al., 2006; Akhtaruddin, 2005; Inchausti, 1997; Cooke, 1989).

With regard to biological assets, prior to IAS 41, "current accounting principles typically do not respond very well to the particular characteristics of agricultural business and the information needs of farmers and their stakeholders" (Argilés and Slof, 2001:361).

Where measurement is concerned, IAS 41 deals with the concept of "living assets", which represents the singular characteristic of natural biological growth that historical cost valuation is unable to manage (Herbohn et al., 1998). The severe change from traditional, historical cost to fair value measurement (Oliveira et al., 2015; Elad and Herbohn, 2011; Lefter and Roman, 2007) has been responsible for the emergence of the debate in agricultural accounting (Argilés et al., 2011).

At first glance, regarding the obligation of IAS 41 to measure biological assets at fair value, it may seem less reasonable to analyse it as a matter of choice. If there are firms that use the unreliability clause of fair value, ideally this should mean that firms are unable to report biological assets at fair value. However, according to some literature, it seems that there are other reasons related to firm and country environment that could explain the adoption of historical cost, even when the clause does not apply (Taplin *et al.*, 2014; Christensen and Nikolaev, 2013; Guo and Yang, 2013; Hlaing and Pourjalali, 2012; Elad and Herbohn, 2011; Daniel *et al.*, 2010; Fisher *et al.*, 2010; Quagli and Avallone, 2010; Muller *et al.*, 2008; Elad, 2004). Therefore, measurement is analysed in this research under accounting choice theory.

### *Literature review*

#### *Disclosure requirements of IAS 41*

There are some studies in the literature that have assessed the implementation impact of IAS 41 (Scherch *et al.*, 2013; Silva *et al.*, 2012; Theiss *et al.*, 2012; Elad and Herbohn, 2011; PricewaterhouseCoopers (PwC), 2011 and 2009).

Elad and Herbohn (2011) conducted a survey in order to determine perceptions from several users of financial information, such as valuation consultants, accountants and auditors from the agricultural sector in Australia, France and the United Kingdom. Based on a checklist of disclosures prescribed by IAS 41 (in which each firm was assigned a score based on the percentage of disclosed items), they concluded that there is a lack of comparability of disclosure practices. French firms (compared to the other two countries) tend not to disclose complete information on biological assets.

PwC (2011 and 2009) conducted two international studies concerning the impact of adopting IAS 41 in the timber sector. The main goal was to provide what might be considered best practices in fair valuation of this sector and related disclosures. In both studies, PwC identified the major pronouncements described in the notes of the financial statements, highlighting some of the main constraints, comparisons and dissimilarities. In general, firms have different levels of transparency regarding biological assets disclosure and they usually do not discuss fair valuation assumptions, so there is an opportunity for further improvement.

Further empirical evidence about disclosure practices relating to this standard is still scarce. For example, the following studies focus on Brazil.

Silva *et al.* (2012) developed a disclosure index concerning the information related to the agricultural sector of 45 Brazilian firms regarding the 2010 annual report. The disclosure of biological asset types and the reconciliation of the carrying value of their changes are the most frequently reported items, but other items are neglected, such as management risks and other constraints of biological assets. Regarding Brazil's adoption of IFRS and a sample of 24 traded Brazilian firms in 2010, Scherch *et al.* (2013) identified that, on average, there was 57% conformity with *Comitê de Pronunciamentos Contábeis (CPC) 29 – Pronunciamento técnico – Ativo Biológico e Produto Agrícola* (equivalent standard to IAS 41 in Brazil). Silva *et al.* (2012) and Scherch *et al.* (2013) both concluded that a higher transparency level in disclosure would help to mitigate information asymmetry.

Similarly, Theiss *et al.* (2012) investigated the implementation of CPC 29 guidelines of 21 Brazilian listed firms in 2010. Using a disclosure index, the results stated that 95% of the sample partially complies with general information on biological assets. The study suggested that some of the information required is considered confidential by the firm's administration. Therefore, disclosure items were not fully disclosed. Consequently, the stakeholders, including auditors and regulators, should play an important role in analysing whether or not the biological assets disclosure is sufficient.

*Measurement requirements of IAS 41*

The choice between fair value and historical cost accounting is one of the most extensively discussed subjects in the literature (Hail *et al.*, 2010; Laux and Leuz, 2010). In the particular case of biological assets, the constraints of implementing the IAS 41 related to fair valuation have been investigated by various authors (Gabriel and Stefea, 2013; Elad and Herbohn, 2011; Argilés *et al.*, 2009; Herbohn and Herbohn, 2006; Argilés and Slof, 2001).

Firstly, Elad and Herbohn (2011) demonstrated a high level of agreement where the costs of measuring biological assets at fair value outweigh the corresponding benefits. This is the case with plantation firms in which the fair value of tropical crops such as rubber trees, oil palms and tea can only be ascertained at excessive costs. Another concern is the apparent need for the auditor to write an audit report on the firms' financial statements that claim "the reader's attention to inherent uncertainties regarding the valuation of biological assets under IAS 41" (Elad and Herbohn, 2011:107).

Additionally, Herbohn and Herbohn (2006) evaluated the impact of IAS 41 on the forestry sector of the accounting standard AASB

(Australian Accounting Standards Board) 1037 – Self-generating and Regenerating Assets, in Australia, as well as the methods of forestry valuation. They highlighted the subjectivity of fair value measurement and the volatility of results related to unrealised gains and losses that are recognised in the income statement. There is a question that remains unanswered: "do such accounting procedures (fair value measurement) reflect the nature of investment in forestry" (Herbohn and Herbohn, 2006:175)?

Furthermore, Gabriel and Stefea (2013) argued that IAS 41 must be carefully analysed in terms of the impact on production forecasting in accounting, the impact on fair value measurement over cash flows and in terms of the possibility of firms using accounting for their own interests. First of all, given the fact that crop production depends on climate conditions, the relevant fair value that is achieved today given specific assumptions may not remain the same the following day. Secondly, the changes in fair value throughout different periods could imply recognition of gains, and moreover, it could determine a loss at the point of harvest. Finally, with regard to the diversity of fair valuation models, managers could choose a specific measurement to serve their own interests.

In order to exemplify such limitations, George (2007), Director of the SIPEF Belgian group (international agro-industrial conglomerate), states that, nowadays, instead of historical cost, there is a permeable concept of fair value which impacts accounting information and complicates auditing opinion. Actually, Deloitte, SIPEF's auditing firm, draws the financial users' attention to the uncertainty caused by the fair value adoption. Consequently, SIPEF isolates such effects, in the financial statements, so that the potential investor can analyse the results before and after fair value adoption.

In spite of previous contributions, Argilés *et al.* (2009) concluded that fair valuation does not imply gain volatility and assures a higher predictive power of future results. They analysed the impact of using fair value in biological assets in Spain, with a sample of about 500 Spanish firms from the agricultural sector. The main conclusion was that fair valuation allows the manager to anticipate financial problems. In addition, the improvement in results precision mitigates agency problems, as managers are perceived as specialised accountants even more.

In order to investigate both issues (disclosure and measurement of biological assets), in addition to IAS 41 requirements, this research adopts two specific segments (firm and country levels) supported by Luft and Shields (2014:555) whereby "reducing the number of plausible alternatives through narrow specification often contributes to the effectiveness and efficiency of research design", which is presented as follows.

## Firm and country-level drivers: Disclosure and measurement

In a conceptual perspective, there are several theories that could explain firm-level drivers of disclosure practices, such as agency theory (Jensen and Meckling, 1976) and signalling theory (Morris, 1987). Additionally, firm-level drivers of measurement practices could be supported by agency theory (Jensen and Meckling, 1976) and accounting choice theory (Fields *et al.*, 2001; Watts, 1992; Zmijewski and Hagerman, 1981). Based on a transversal perspective, contingency theory supports country-level drivers of disclosure and measurement practices (Doupnik and Salter, 1995).

Agency theory defines the incentive problems in firms motivated by ownership and control separation – the principal (owner of the firm) and the agent (manager) problem (Jensen and Meckling, 1976). In this sense, where disclosure practices are concerned, managers are strongly motivated to disclose complete information in order to achieve their compensation. For example, larger firms are expected to have higher agency costs; therefore, these firms are also encouraged to improve the level of information given to stakeholders and financial analysts. Consistent with the previous considerations, signalling theory is implied by positive monitoring costs in agency theory (Morris, 1987). Under information asymmetry, a firm that is listed on several stock exchanges which develops international trading activities has more information to control, and consequently is interested in communicating its position to stakeholders by improving disclosure.

Regarding accounting choices, the related theory comprises the firm's manager's choice of one accounting method over another (Watts, 1992), which corresponds in this study to choosing between fair value and historical cost as a valuation method. Given market imperfections such as transaction costs and externalities, Fields *et al.* (2001) stated that accounting choices are used by managers to disseminate their private information and to influence the beliefs of rational investors. Moreover, accounting choice could detect the economic determinants that move managers towards certain directions (Zmijewski and Hagerman, 1981) and could explain how these determinants could be changed. This would be particularly helpful for accounting regulators to anticipate, for example, how firms would answer to a change in accounting rules.

With regard to contingency theory, according to Doupnik and Salter (1995), the external environment, the institutional structure and the cultural values support accounting divergence between countries. The external environment comprises various factors, namely: the legal system, the relationship between businesses and providers of capital, tax laws, inflation levels, political and economic ties, the level of education and the level of economic development. For example, referring to the present study, the legal system (belonging to a code law versus a common law country) and the relationship between tax rules and accounting (strong or weak) both have an impact on the extent of disclosure and on fair value adoption.

Based on these theories, this research explores several drivers that are expected to be related to the disclosure level and measurement type. The selected variables are supported by other studies that also focus on disclosure and measurement practices in general. Therefore, this study aims to assess whether the same expectations and results are obtained in the particular context of biological assets. For each independent variable, the causal mechanisms and the supporting theories are identified and explained as follows.

### *Firm-level variables: Disclosure*

The research explores several firm-level drivers that are expected to be related to the disclosure level, such as biological assets intensity, ownership concentration, firm size, auditor type, internationalisation level, listing status, profitability and sector.

### *Biological assets intensity*

Considering other non-financial assets, for example goodwill impairment, firms have a higher propensity to disclose when they have larger amounts of non-financial assets (Amiraslani *et al.*, 2013; Heitzman *et al.*, 2010). Moreover, goodwill impairment requires valuation skills, so there is also a strong expectation that firms allocate more resources to improve quality reporting when they have a relative materiality position (Glaum *et al.*, 2013; Shalev, 2009). That could be the case with biological assets, given the complexity of disclosure requirements.

Regarding stakeholder theory, Silva *et al.* (2012) expect preparers of financial reporting of biological assets to assure the disclosure level regulated by IAS 41, in order to provide information to users of such financial statements. This statement is even more significant if firms have material amounts of biological assets. In fact, Scherch *et al.* (2013) state that the disclosure level rises with the increasing intensity of biological assets.

The above considerations indicate an expected positive association between the intensity of biological assets and the extent of mandatory and voluntary disclosure concerning biological assets.

### Ownership concentration

The firms' reporting incentives are influenced by ownership structure (Glaum *et al.*, 2013; Leuz, 2010). Considering the fact that agency problems arise because of the separation of ownership and control (Jensen and Meckling, 1976), agency costs increase as the ownership structure becomes more dispersed (Fama and Jensen, 1983). In order to decrease agency costs, firms with higher ownership diffusion have stronger incentives to provide transparent financial reporting (Oliveira *et al.*, 2006).

In addition, IFRS are settled to ensure that information is provided to shareholders in order to decrease information asymmetry between managers and external users and to enhance disclosure transparency (Ding *et al.*, 2007). For firms that are controlled by several investors, higher demand for public disclosure may also lead to higher incentives for disclosure (Daske *et al.*, 2013).

The above considerations indicate an expected negative association between ownership concentration and the extent of mandatory and voluntary disclosure concerning biological assets.

### Firm size

Some studies indicate firm size as a determinant of compliance with reporting standards (Amiraslani *et al.*, 2013; Glaum *et al.*, 2013; Oliveira *et al.*, 2006). Glaum *et al.* (2013) demonstrated that larger firms are responsible for disclosing financial information with more quality than smaller firms, since the former usually have more resources allocated to accounting divisions. Furthermore, the costs of increased disclosure are well supported by larger firms (Amiraslani *et al.*, 2013).

Larger firms are likely to have a higher percentage of outside capital and enlarged agency costs (Jensen and Meckling, 1976). Consequently, these firms are required to assure a more developed level of information to stakeholders, especially to financial analysts (Depoers, 2000).

The above considerations indicate an expected positive association between firm size and the extent of mandatory and voluntary disclosure concerning biological assets.

*Auditor type*

Auditing is an effective function of restraining managers' opportunistic reporting conduct (Tsalavoutas, 2011). Consequently, regarding agency theory, independent auditors reduce agency costs (Jensen and Meckling, 1976). Watts and Zimmerman (1983:615) emphasised that it is possible "(...) only if the market expects the auditor to have a nonzero level of independence". Committees and penalties, including reputation loss, are some of the incentives for auditors to assure their independence. In order to avoid reputation costs, these firms demand a higher disclosure level (Oliveira *et al.*, 2006; Chalmers and Godfrey, 2004).

Furthermore, prior literature explains the strength of enforcement of accounting standards by the existence of stronger auditing firms (Hope, 2003). The larger the auditing firm, the higher is its perceived quality (DeAngelo, 1981). Several studies have revealed a positive association between disclosure level and being audited by the Big 4 auditing firms (Glaum *et al.*, 2013; Cascino and Gassen, 2011; Hodgdon *et al.*, 2009).

The above considerations indicate an expected positive association between auditor type and the extent of mandatory and voluntary disclosure concerning biological assets.

*Internationalisation level and listing status*

The disclosure level is positively related to the degree of foreign activity in the firm (Amiraslani *et al.*, 2013; Daske *et al.*, 2013) and to the firm's listing status (Amiraslani *et al.*, 2013; Cooke, 1992). Managers of firms that operate in several geographical areas have to provide larger disclosure, bearing in mind the higher complexity of the firms' activities (Cooke, 1989).

With signalling theory, international trading activities (Oliveira *et al.*, 2006; Depoers, 2000) on several stock exchanges (Oliveira *et al.*, 2006; Hope, 2003) imply large and complex amounts of information to control. Consequently, this influences firms to express their international position to stakeholders by improving disclosure.

The above considerations indicate an expected positive association between the internationalisation level and the extent of mandatory and voluntary disclosure concerning biological assets.

*Profitability*

Taking into consideration agency theory (Jensen and Meckling, 1976), disclosure controls a manager's performance. Managers disclose detailed information in order to assure their compensation and position. Additionally, signalling theory explains that when the rate of return is high, firms are expected to disclose good news to prevent any reduction of their share value (Oliveira *et al.*, 2006).

Lan *et al.* (2013) and Chavent *et al.* (2006) considered firm performance, measured by the return on equity, as a relevant explanatory variable for the disclosure level. Lang and Lundholm (1993:250) noticed that "the results from theoretical and empirical research suggest disclosure could be increasing, constant, or even decreasing in firm performance". As an example, in the case of negative earnings information, firms are more likely to disclose information in order to reduce the possibility of legal liability.

Because of the mixed empirical evidence in prior literature, there is no strong expectation regarding the association between profitability and the extent of mandatory and voluntary disclosure concerning biological assets.

*Sector*

Based on signalling theory, it is expected that firms belonging to the same sector are concerned with assuring the same disclosure level in order to prevent an undesirable assessment by the market (Oliveira *et al.*, 2006). As a consequence, firms tend to be motivated to follow their corresponding sector practice (Amiraslani *et al.*, 2013). With regard to legitimacy theory, and in response to stimulating requirements of IFRS reporting, firms may follow common industry practices to legitimise their performance (Glaum *et al.*, 2013).

In terms of mandatory disclosure, Rahman *et al.* (2002) compared accounting regulations and accounting practices in Australia and New Zealand and concluded that sector influences the disclosure level.

The above considerations indicate an expected positive association between the following sectors (agriculture, forestry, fishing and mining sectors and in the manufacturing sector, as these are associated with biological assets) and the extent of mandatory and voluntary disclosure concerning biological assets.

**Firm-level variables: Measurement**

Due to the lack of studies on firm-level drivers of biological assets measurement, this research has relied on literature where the topic of examining these drivers is discussed for other non-financial assets, such as investment property and property, plant and equipment as summarised in Table 3.1. They have some of the drivers in common that explain the adoption of fair value for non-financial assets and also the applied methodology: the binary models.

The research explores several firm-level drivers that are expected to be related to the measurement type, namely: biological assets intensity, firm size, listing status, regulation expertise, potential growth, leverage and sector.

*Biological assets intensity*

As far as non-financial assets are concerned, in general, Daniel *et al.* (2010) conclude that firms tend to adopt fair value and therefore assure more value-relevant[1] information to investors when the intensity of non-financial assets is high. For property, plant and equipment, Christensen and Nikolaev (2013) and Hlaing and Pourjalali (2012) found that the likelihood of using fair value increases with the proportion of these assets to total assets, meaning that the costs of fair value outweigh the benefits when an asset represents a slight percentage of the statement of financial position.

The above considerations suggest that firms with a higher biological assets intensity are more likely to use the fair value measurement model, avoiding the use of the unreliability clause.

*Firm size*

Regarding the positive theory of accounting policy choice, Zmijewski and Hagerman (1981) concluded that size is significantly linked to the choice of a firm's income strategy. Moreover, larger firms denote higher agency costs (Jensen and Meckling, 1976) and equally have the required resources and desirable motivations to act in accordance with accounting standards (Cairns *et al.*, 2011), which in this study means measuring biological assets at fair value.

In terms of non-financial assets, Daniel *et al.* (2010) present two opposite perspectives related to firm size. On the one hand, smaller firms are expected to be more reluctant when choosing fair value because the implicit cost is higher for them. On the other hand, smaller firms could be inclined to adopt fair value in order to reduce the information asymmetry between investors and managers. Quagli and Avallone (2010) also confirm that the variable size, as a proxy to political costs, reduces the likelihood of using fair value in investment property.

*Table 3.1.* Measurement – firm-level drivers

| Paper | Assets | Selection | Variables | Main conclusions |
|---|---|---|---|---|
| Taplin *et al.* (2014) | Investment property | 96 listed firms (randomly selected) China 2008 | Leverage (book value of total liabilities divided by book value of total assets)<br><br>Listing status (dummy variable coded 1 if the firm is internationally listed)<br><br>International revenue (dummy variable coded 1 if the firm reports revenue from international sources)<br><br>Earnings management (ratio of the standard deviation of operating income divided by the standard deviation of cash flow from the operation)<br><br>Ownership concentration (% of shares outstanding that are held by directors) | Less evidence supports the usage of the fair value model for firms with higher leverage.<br><br>Listed firms overseas, with international operations and higher volatility of reported earnings, are more likely to use the fair value model.<br><br>Firms with more dispersed ownership tend to adopt fair value in order to reduce information asymmetry. |
| Christensen and Nikolaev (2013) | Investment property | 275 firms United Kingdom, Germany 2005 | Country (dummy variable coded 1 if the firm is domiciled in this country)<br><br>CountrySic65 (dummy variable coded 1 if the firm has sic-code 65 (real estate) among its first five sic-code classifications)<br><br>Leverage (total liabilities divided by market value of assets) | Fair value adoption is influenced by: Institutional differences.<br><br>Measures ability to improve firm performance (which is related to how an asset is used, to hold or to trade it).<br><br>The cost of calculating fair value, conversely related to the asset's liquidity, is the main reason for managers to avoid fair value. |

| | | | |
|---|---|---|---|
| Hlaing and Pourjalali (2012) | Property, plant and equipment | 232 firms United States of America 2004–2007 | Size (logarithm of the total assets) Tangibility (ratio of total net property, plant and equipment to total assets) Leverage (ratio of long-term debt to total assets) | Larger firms, with higher ratio of the total amount of property, plant and equipment to total assets, are more likely to use the fair value model. Non-financial assets can be revaluated under manager discretion, in order to influence investors' decisions, and for that reason, the reliability of this measurement is controversial. |
| Quagli and Avallone (2010) | Investment property | 76 firms Finland, France, Germany, Greece, Italy, Spain, Sweden 2005–2007 | Size (logarithm of the total assets) Leverage (debt-to-asset ratio) Market-to-book value (market-to-book ratio) Earnings smoothing (dummy variable coded 1 if the firm has an earnings smoothing index higher than the average index of earnings smoothing in firm's country of domicile) | Contractual efficiency, information asymmetry and managerial opportunism are drivers of fair value. As proxies of contractual efficiency, size reduces the fair value choice and leverage does not seem to influence it. Market-to-book ratio and earnings smoothing measure information asymmetry and managerial opportunism, respectively; both influence fair value choice negatively. |

(continued)

Table 3.1. (cont.)

| Paper | Assets | Selection | Variables | Main conclusions |
|---|---|---|---|---|
| Daniel et al. (2010) | Non-financial assets | Chief Financial Officers (CFO) US public firms 2008 | Size (logarithm of the market value of equity) Tangibility (ratio of the property, plant and equipment to total assets) Expertise (measured as level 2 and level 3 assets scaled by total assets – both valuations for assets and liabilities are more difficult and costly, given the absence of liquid markets, as previously explained) Leverage (long-term debt divided by total equity) | Larger firms; higher ratio of non-financial assets to total assets; higher expertise in fair value measurements; and more leveraged firms are drivers of fair value for non-financial assets. Fair value adoption is related to the corresponding benefits and costs: this trade-off could be reflected in the cost of equity or debt capital of the firm and consequently could assure a better firm performance. |
| Muller et al. (2008) | Investment property | 77 real estate firms Continental Europe 2004–2006 | Tangibility (ratio of the investment property to total assets) Ownership concentration (% of the stock held by insiders of the firm) International operations (% of the revenue generated from operations outside of the firm's country of domicile) IFRS adoption indicator (dummy variable coded 1 if the firm adopts IFRS voluntarily prior to the mandatory adoption effective 2005) | Fair value has been adopted for investment property, prior to IAS 40 mandatory adoption, when there was a higher investor demand for this information and also a greater commitment to assure financial reporting transparency. Evidence suggests that market participants distinguish diversity in the quality of fair value disclosure, even when this practice is followed under a required standard. |

Because of the mixed empirical evidence in prior literature, there is no strong expectation regarding the association between firm size and use of the fair value measurement model.

## Listing status

Stock exchange is the "primary enforcer of accounting standards" and it is seen as a "managerial choice variable(s)" (Hope, 2003:244). Daniel *et al.* (2010) state that firms with higher levels of international operations are more interested in fair market valuations arising from their international counterparts.

The economic inferences of accounting choices grabbed the attention of researchers (Fields *et al.*, 2001). Taplin *et al.* (2014) focused on a group of economic motivations in order to explain the drivers of fair valuation for investment property. For example, they confirmed that Chinese firms listed on foreign stock exchanges are expected to use fair value for this type of asset.

The above considerations suggest that firms that are listed on one (or more) foreign stock exchanges are more likely to use the fair value measurement model, avoiding use of the unreliability clause.

## Regulation expertise

With regard to IFRS adoption, "as opposed to rules-based systems, accounting standards of the principles persuasion do not address every controversial issue at hand but keep considerable ambiguity about such major processes as record keeping and measurement" (Carmona and Trombeta, 2008:456). Therefore, this principle-based system assures a change in accountants' skills and qualifications. Taking the measurement of biological assets into consideration, a higher level of regulation expertise would facilitate recognition of fair value.

For example, for fair value measurement of non-financial assets in general, Daniel *et al.* (2010) argue that firms with more level 2 and level 3 inputs are more likely to choose the fair value option. Both level valuations are more complex and costly regarding the absence of liquid markets. Consequently, these firms already have experience in estimating fair value and are expected to be more receptive to this measurement.

The above considerations suggest that firms that have higher regulation expertise are more likely to use the fair value measurement model, avoiding use of the unreliability clause.

*Potential growth*

Growth opportunities have a potential effect on managers' accounting choices (Daniel *et al.*, 2010). Firms include assets-in-place, with perceptible value and investment opportunities, and with a value that is subject to discretionary judgments (Myers, 1977). Two different perspectives are addressed by Missonier-Piera (2007). Firstly, firms that have more growth opportunities than assets-in-place are expected to have a lower probability of revaluating their assets comparatively to firms with more assets-in-place. This happens because revaluating assets is usually associated to fixed assets. Secondly, and regarding information asymmetry, firms with more growth prospects than assets-in-place are more familiar with their value than investors. Besides, controlling the activities of these firms is more challenging than controlling activities from firms composed mainly of assets-in-place. As such, and taking into account agency theory, firms are more willing to revalue fixed assets in order to reduce information asymmetry with potential investors.

Because of the mixed empirical evidence in prior literature, there is no strong expectation regarding the association between potential growth and use of the fair value measurement model.

*Leverage*

Regarding accounting choice theory, Fields *et al.* (2001) explain that contractual motivations mitigate agency costs due to the fact that settled contractual engagements ensure fewer conflicts between agents. In particular, managers tend to increase their compensation and decrease the probability of bond covenant violations by choosing accounting methods (Fields *et al.*, 2001). Therefore, the higher the ratio between debt and equity, the higher the propensity of managers to follow strategies to increase income (Watts and Zimmerman, 1990). For example, in terms of investment property, Christensen and Nikolaev (2013) found that leverage is a key determinant for fair value measurement.

The above considerations suggest that firms with a higher leverage level are more likely to use the fair value measurement model, avoiding use of the unreliability clause.

*Sector*

As far as industry impact is concerned, Watts (1992) contends that accounting choice also varies according to different sectors. In particular, the contractual engagements are established based on a cost-benefit analysis. As the costs of such affairs change from sector to sector, accounting procedures also differ between industries. For Fields *et al.* (2001), market imperfections are also responsible for a manager's accounting choice, namely agency costs, information asymmetries and externalities that influence non-contracting parties. One example of an externality is the pressure of industry organisations. Regulating accounting will assure a positive effect on the corresponding externality.

In a study supporting the fact that the financial industry is willing to adopt new norms, Demaria and Dufour (2007) confirm that the financial sector is linked to IFRS choices in the French domain. Contrary to the present study, the above considerations suggest that firms that belong to the following sectors (agriculture, forestry, fishing, mining and manufacturing sectors, as these are associated with biological assets) are more likely to use the fair value measurement model, avoiding use of the unreliability clause.

### Country-level variables

#### Country classification

Even though the aim of IFRS is to assure accounting comparability between countries, it does not eradicate the national, industry and firm-level institutional influences (Wysocki, 2011). Taking the institutional factor into consideration as the main influence for firms' reporting practices (Wysocki, 2011; Nobes, 2008; Djankov *et al.*, 2003), some countries' classifications were developed in the literature (Brown *et al.*, 2014; Kaufmann *et al.*, 2011; Leuz, 2010; Nobes, 2008; La Porta *et al.*, 1998).

La Porta *et al.* (1998) analysed legal rules related to shareholders and its origin and the quality of enforcement in 49 countries. They categorised the firms by common law and code law country classification. Nobes (2008) categorised countries into two groups, namely "strong equity, commercially-driven" (for example, the Netherlands and the United Kingdom) and "weak equity, government-driven and tax-dominated" (for example, Germany, France and Italy).

Nowadays, there are other classifications, for example, cluster classification (Leuz, 2010) using regulatory and reporting practice variables. Based on regulatory and reporting practice variables, Leuz (2010) suggested that outsider economies with large and developed stock markets, dispersed ownership, strong investor protection and strong enforcement (cluster 1) show higher disclosure scores and more informative earnings than insider economies with less-developed stock markets, concentrated ownership and weak investor protection. Insider economies are divided into two clusters, diverging in the strength of their legal systems. As a result, those economies with strong enforcement (cluster 2) show higher transparency scores than the others (cluster 3). Annex A presents Leuz's (2010) cluster classification.

Given worldwide governance indicators, Kaufmann *et al.* (2011) supported a common set of proxies based on responses to surveys that captured the differences between countries on various matters including rule of law, regulatory effectiveness, control of corruption, voice and accountability, political stability and government effectiveness. They measured the perceptions of the extent to which market participants have confidence in and comply with the laws of society (Preiato *et al.*, 2015). Rule of law and regulatory quality are two examples, as follows: rule of law corresponds to "capturing perceptions of the extent to which agents have confidence in and abide by the rules of society, and in particular the quality of contract enforcement, property rights, the police, and the courts, as well as the likelihood of crime and violence" (Kaufmann *et al.*, 2011: 223); regulatory quality corresponds to "capturing perceptions of the ability of the government to formulate and implement sound policies and regulations that permit and promote private sector development" (Kaufmann *et al.*, 2011: 223).

Empirical evidence corroborates that the paradigm is changing. Apparently, Germany is moving from the Continental European accounting model to a middle position between this one and the Anglo-American accounting model (Hellmann *et al.*, 2013). The promulgation of the Act to Modernize Accounting Law (issued in May 2009) had an impact on accounting principles, such as to settle new recognition and valuation rules and to eliminate the straight liaison to tax rules. In addition, instead of being considered a common law country, the United Kingdom should be included in the European accounting model (Callao Gastón *et al.*, 2010; Lewis and Salter, 2006).

More recent country classifications involve other proxies, such as auditing and enforcement, both of which are related to IFRS adoption.

Improving transparency, lowering the costs of capital and cross-country investments, improving the comparability of financial reports and attention of foreign analysts are well-known benefits of the adoption of IFRS, which are all supported by earlier studies (George *et al.*, 2016). All of the benefits tend to diverge considerably across countries and firms. Currently, this divergence is mostly linked to changes in enforcement. Stefano and Gassen (2015) documented that the firms from countries with higher reporting enforcement exhibit larger comparability effects of mandatory IFRS adoption.

Based on previous considerations, Brown *et al.* (2014) proposed an index that measures the quality of auditors' work and the degree of accounting enforcement by independent enforcement bodies, in order to capture institutional differences between countries that are relevant for financial reporting. The authors used data from the World Bank, the International Federation of Accounts, Fédération des Experts Comptables Européens and national securities regulators and calculated three indices for 51 countries for 2002, 2005, and 2008, namely: audit proxy, enforcement proxy and a combination between audit and enforcement proxy. This approach assigned 0, 1 and 2 scores to each item in order to obtain a ranking of countries. By calculating this index for three years, the authors showed how a country's position changed over the study period and how countries are ranked relative to their peers. Annex B presents this classification.

Overall, the attempt to classify accounting systems has been a familiar issue in accounting research (Nobes and Stadler, 2013). Country classification is one possible approach. A country-level variable "may act as a summary measure for a country's approach to a number of regulatory issues and therefore could have significant explanatory power in regressions involving institutional (or country) variables" (Leuz, 2010:242). In the context of disclosure and measurement, this research explores one country-level driver, legal status, which is examined by different classifications.

### Country-level variable: Disclosure

Due to the diversity of country classifications, as a first step, this research adopts two approaches, namely the dichotomy of common law versus code law countries and cluster classifications. Regarding the first classification, firms that belong to common law countries are expected to converge to IFRS (Nobes, 2008) and to improve their accounting quality (La Porta *et al.*, 1998). According to Leuz's (2010) cluster classification, three clusters are considered, as previously mentioned: outsider economies (cluster 1), insider economies with better legal enforcement systems (cluster 2) and insider economies with weaker legal enforcement systems (cluster 3). Firms that belong to cluster 1 tend to show a higher disclosure level.

Regarding the fact that disclosure practices under discussion in this study include mandatory and voluntary disclosure requirements of IAS 41, the above considerations indicate an expected positive association between firms that belong to the following branches: common law and cluster 1 and the extent of mandatory and voluntary disclosure concerning biological assets.

Additionally, this research also adopts the approach suggested by Brown *et al.* (2014), in which country classification is based on auditing and enforcement proxies. In particular, Preiato *et al.* (2015) tested the new enforcement proxies from Brown *et al.* (2014), measuring differences between countries, and concluded that those measures improve explanatory power when compared to alternative measures, such as: dichotomy of common law versus code law countries (La Porta *et al.*, 1998); World Bank indicators (Kaufmann *et al.*, 2011); World Economic Forum proxies (2008; 2010) and resourcing of Security Market Regulations (Jackson and Roe, 2009).

Therefore, it is expected that audit and enforcement proxies from Brown *et al.* (2014) have more influence than the dichotomy of common law versus code law countries (La Porta *et al.*, 1998) or cluster classification (Leuz, 2010) in explaining the differences in disclosure levels on biological assets among listed firms.

### *Country-level variable: Measurement*

Several international studies deal with the influence of the country origin on biological assets measurement (Guo and Yang, 2013; Elad and Herbohn, 2011; Fisher *et al.*, 2010; Elad, 2004).

Elad and Herbohn (2011) concluded that firms from Australia and the United Kingdom (common law countries) are fair value adopters, while in French firms (code law country) historical cost is the commonly used method.

Regarding another common law country, New Zealand, Fisher *et al.* (2010) identified listed firms with biological assets for which there were limited or no active markets and have no applied historical cost. This may suggest that fair valuation in this context does not appear to be a problem.

Elad (2004) provided a worldwide comparison between Europe, Africa and Australia. The study concluded that fair value is more suitable than historical cost for those biological assets that have an active market and is more comprehensible for the users of the information. African countries do not seem to apply fair value, whereas Australian countries are followers of fair value, although they have identified a large volatility related to the fair valuation of biological assets.

Finally, and regarding a specific country such as China, Guo and Yang (2013) argue that biological assets measurement is affected by the comprehensiveness of the assets' nature, the market environment and the balance between the relevance and reliability of accounting information. Although the existence of a mature market and regulatory environment is suitable for fair valuation, it could also motivate performance manipulation. Currently, in this country the historical cost is desirable when compared to fair value. However, as markets become more mature and active, it is expected that fair value will replace historical cost.

Instead of adopting any pre-determined classification, the present research follows a worldwide governance indicator by Kaufmann *et al.* (2011) which was previously introduced: regulatory quality. Recently, Lindahl and Schadéwitz (2013) questioned the relevance of the law variable in financial reporting practices used by La Porta *et al.* (1998). Based on this finding, regulatory quality was preferred against rule of law. The above considerations suggest that firms that have a higher level of regulatory quality are more likely to use the fair value measurement model, avoiding use of the unreliability clause.

After presenting the state of the art and identifying the firm and country-level drivers that explain disclosure and measurement practices of biological assets, the next section operationalises the disclosure approach, introducing a well-known instrument: the disclosure index.

## Disclosure index

Studies on disclosure rely on the definition and measurement of the disclosure index. Regarding voluntary disclosure, there are several papers that include both the extent-based and the quality-based analysis related to the corresponding topic of interest (Abraham and Shrives, 2014; Bellora and Guenther, 2013; Hooks and Van Staden, 2011; Van Staden and Hooks, 2007). According to Hooks and Van Staden (2011), the first analysis quantifies the extent of reporting on a specific issue using several measures such as words, sentences or pages and the second analysis evaluates the quality of the disclosures using a quality index. There are several limitations when it comes to the extent-based analysis. For example, Steenkamp and Northcott (2007) stated that the researcher's role is crucial in establishing what information is materialised from a content analysis. In spite of the focus being the text, it can be interpreted in several ways. Moreover, the scope of the analysed text is delimited by its context. Marston and Shrives (1991) stated that there are repetitions of specific words in the annual reports and that firms differ in the complexity of their operations, which can lead to the conclusion that measuring information by counting numbers or words is not the ideal solution.

Considering mandatory disclosure and compliance with goodwill impairment disclosures, Amiraslani *et al.* (2013) concluded that there is an excessive use of boilerplate language combined with the wording being restated from the corresponding standard, exercising a minimum level of judgment.[2] With the purpose of mitigating these boilerplate disclosures, Hans Hoogervorst, Chairman of the IASB at the IFRS Foundation conference on 27 June 2013, encouraged excluding non-material disclosures related to "less is often more", avoiding the risk of annual reports turning into merely compliance documents rather than a means of communication (IFRS Foundation, 2013).

Given the previous clarification and the fact that more disclosure may not be synonymous with higher disclosure quality, the present study adopts a quality-based analysis. Therefore, based on prior research (Lan *et al.*, 2013; Santos *et al.*, 2013; Lopes and Rodrigues, 2007; Oliveira *et al.*, 2006; Akhtaruddin, 2005; Owusu-Ansah, 1998; Inchausti, 1997), this book includes a disclosure index, which will be explored in Chapter 5, that covers empirical evidence worldwide. In order to corroborate this option with regard to biological assets, Scherch *et al.* (2013), Silva *et al.* (2012), Theiss *et al.* (2012) also considered a disclosure index within a Brazilian context.

## Notes

1  According to Barth and Clinch (1998:200), "value relevant" means that "the amount has a significant relation in the predicted direction with share prices or the non-market-based estimate of firm value".
2  According to Hans Hoogervorst (which is also supported by empirical evidence), sometimes firms copy the paragraphs of the standards instead of disclosing in-depth information related to their activity.

# 4 Fair value relevance of biological assets

## Introduction

Fair value relevance is a widely discussed issue in the literature (Mala and Chand, 2012; Laux and Leuz, 2010; Hitz, 2007; Ball, 2006; Cairns, 2006; Barlev and Haddad, 2003; Barth *et al.*, 2001; Holthausen and Watts, 2001). Even though fair value is responsible for the volatility of results and for stimulating some managerial discretion, it incorporates more information into financial statements. In this chapter, in order to explore the investors' perception of this additional information, it is important to differentiate recognition and disclosure, given previous considerations about disclosure and measurement (Kun, 2013; Ahmed *et al.*, 2006; Ball, 2006; Davis-Friday *et al.*, 1999). Both are a means of assuring the decision-usefulness of financial statement information (Badenhorst *et al.*, 2015). According to Choudhary (2011) and Al Jifri and Citron (2009), recognised values settled by managers and revised by auditors have different requirements when compared to disclosed values. Consequently, investors and accounting regulators value recognised values more than disclosed ones. This is especially useful for standard setters when deciding between recognition and disclosure.

Most of the academic literature on this topic is addressed in the context of financial instruments. Consideration of fair value relevance in other fields is much less common. This chapter focuses this topic under IAS 41 in order to enhance knowledge within the realm of agriculture, given the fact that "IAS 41 is a 'true' fair value standard: the fair value of biological assets is reported on the firm's balance sheet and any change in the fair value of the biological assets over the reporting period is recognized in the periodic income as an unrealized gain or loss" (Huffman, 2013:2).

Some evidence supports the idea that fair value is more reliable in the decision-making process of agents within the realm of agriculture (Argilés Bosh *et al.*, 2012). However, the standardisation assured by IAS 41 in this domain is not capable of mitigating the subjective process of fair valuation (Machado *et al.*, 2015). The main disadvantage of fair value is the absence of active markets for some biological assets. With regard to the diversity of fair valuation models, it is possible for firms to use accounting for their own interests (Gabriel and Stefea, 2013). Moreover, Martins *et al.* (2012) highlight that each biological asset has its own attributes and life-cycles, which means that the corresponding valuation is more difficult to achieve.

## Literature review

### *Fair value relevance under international financial reporting*

Value relevance research makes inferences as to how accounting information is reflected in the share prices and influences investors' decision-making (Barth *et al.*, 2001). Adding more information into financial statements seems to be the most important advantage of fair value accounting (Mala and Chand, 2012; Ball, 2006; Barlev and Haddad, 2003; Barth *et al.*, 2001). In particular, fair value covers more information than historical cost whenever there is either an observable market price that managers cannot adjust or an independently observable and reliable estimate of market price (Ball, 2006).

Nevertheless, there are also some well-known disadvantages related to fair value accounting. The recognised fair value changes in capital or in profit and loss are responsible for the higher volatility of reported results, hiding the value creation process (Mala and Chand, 2012). Even though volatility becomes a disadvantage to investors if it represents managerial discretion, Ball (2006) also contended that volatility should not be a problem whenever it reproduces timely incorporation of new information in earnings.

Some authors go further in the criticism by supporting the idea that fair value accounting may have been responsible for the recent financial crisis. Laux and Leuz (2010) argue that because fair value-based models may not be reliable, fair value accounting may have contributed to the procyclicality of the financial system, exacerbating inherent fluctuations and, in severe cases, causing a downward spiral in financial markets.

Additionally, when a liquid market price is not available, "mark to market" accounting leads to "mark to model" accounting, with several valuation models, such as the present value (discounted cash flow) method and the methods adapted from the original Black-Scholes model (Black and Scholes, 1973). These fair value models are based on specific parameters and assumptions that could lead to management manipulation (Mala and Chand, 2012; Hitz, 2007; Ball, 2006). In fact, given fair value measurement, Fargher and Zhang (2014) stated that when accounting standards allow for managerial discretion, this opportunity is unscrupulously used by managers in practice and will compromise the relevance of financial reporting. Therefore, if users of financial information consider the corresponding information to be unreliable, they will not value this information as meaningful (Fargher and Zhang, 2014). Even though a liquid market price is able to reduce the opportunity for discretion by managers, Ball (2006) highlighted that market liquidity could also lead to another problem when the spreads are high enough to raise uncertainty about fair value in financial statements.

For non-financial assets, such as investment property and biological assets, occasionally a market price is not available, which makes fair value assessment more difficult. Fair value relevance of non-financial assets and biological assets, in particular, will be explained in the next section.

### Fair value relevance of non-financial assets

Several papers discuss the impact of accounting information on investors' decision-making, where biological assets are concerned. The results show no consensus. (Huffman, 2013; Argilés Bosch et al., 2012; Martins et al. 2012; Argilés et al., 2011).

Given a sample of 45 firms from European countries in 2008, Martins et al. (2012) concluded that fair value accounting is recognised as irrelevant in the area of biological assets in terms of the impact that accounting information has on investors' decision-making. They are more interested in the firms' financial performance as a whole. Conversely, through an experiment with students, farmers and accountants engaged in the agricultural sector in Spain, Argilés Bosch et al. (2012) matched the constraints that arise from measuring both valuation methods for biological assets, historical cost and fair value. The findings suggest that fair value is more reliable in the decision-making process of agents in the agricultural sector. Moreover, fair value seems to be more suitable for accounting preparation than historical cost. Argilés et al. (2011) suggested that less reliable measurement under fair value would be expected, since market prices reflect significant variations in the agricultural sector. Based on a sample of 347 Spanish firms from 1995 to 2006 (considering the importance of random factors derived from climate and market conditions in agriculture), the empirical evidence supports there being no difference in the relevance of accounting information from both valuation methods. In this sense, fair value is not responsible for higher unpredictability and volatility for future earnings and cash flows.

In contrast to previous academic discussion concerning asset measurement, which focuses exclusively on fair value or historical cost, Huffman (2013) examined whether asset measurement related to asset use assures more value-relevant information to investors. Regarding generated value, an asset can be classified as an in-exchange asset, which represents a consumable biological asset (for example, a plantation to produce timber logs) or as an in-use asset, which represents a bearer biological asset (for example, a plantation to produce palm oil). Previously, Littleton (1935) stated that the information is more relevant for investors if fair value is applied to in-exchange assets and historical cost is applied to in-use assets. Based on a sample of 183 international firms from 35 countries that adopted IAS 41 in 1999–2001 and 2007–2010, Huffman (2013) concluded that book value and earnings information is more value relevant when consumable biological assets are measured at fair value and bearer biological assets are measured at historical cost.

Because there are few studies on fair value accounting concerning biological assets measurement and the scope of the studies is narrow, generally focusing on comparison between historical cost and fair value, this chapter has also relied on literature where this topic is discussed for other non-financial assets (Baboukardos and Rimmel, 2014; Hamberg and Beisland, 2014; Tsoligkas and Tsalavoutas, 2011; Oliveira *et al.*, 2010; Lourenço and Curto, 2008; Barth and Clinch, 1998), such as goodwill, investment property, research and development (R&D) expenditure, tangible and intangible assets. Table 4.1 summarises the analysed papers. In order to test market valuation implications, all papers have the applied methodology in common; an adaptation of the Ohlson model (Ohlson, 1995). This is further explained in the next chapter and explores worldwide evidence, with the exception of Hamberg and Beisland (2014), which adopts a typical return model. Overall, non-financial assets measured at fair value are value relevant and sometimes this evidence occurs independently of the country classification (common law or code law). Some papers suggest that corresponding mandatory disclosure is also a disciplinary element of the market's perception. Moreover, in the absence of a market price, managers usually act in self-interest.

Table 4.1. Fair value relevance – literature review

| Paper | Assets | Selection | Topics | Main conclusions |
|-------|--------|-----------|--------|------------------|
| Baboukardos and Rimmel (2014) | Goodwill | 76 firms Greece 2014 | Purchased goodwill under IFRS is value relevant. There is a difference in goodwill's value relevance between firms with high and low disclosure level compliance under IFRS. | Fair value measurement of goodwill under IFRS assures relevant information in Greece (code law country). For firms with high (low) disclosure compliance under IFRS, goodwill has a strong effect (no effect) on the equities' market valuation. |
| Hamberg and Beisland (2014) | Goodwill | 2,052 firm-year observations Sweden 2001–2010 | Goodwill amortisations determined under Swedish Generally Accepted Accounting Principles (GAAP) are not value relevant. Value relevance of goodwill impairments determined under Swedish GAAP differs from value relevance of goodwill impairments settled under IFRS 3 – Business Combinations. | Goodwill amortisations are not associated with stock returns. Conversely, the period before IFRS adoption, impairments are no longer statistically related under IFRS 3 (impairment is perceived as a decreased value by market participants when it occurs in addition to amortisations and managers are motivated to prevent the impairment of goodwill). |
| Tsoligkas and Tsalavoutas (2011) | R&D expenditure | 418 firm-year observations United Kingdom 2005–2007 | Capitalised and expensed R&D expenditure are value relevant in the United Kingdom, after 2005. There are different valuation effects of R&D reporting between large and small firms in the United Kingdom, after 2005. | There is a positive (negative) and significant association between capitalised (expensed) R&D and market values. R&D expenses are negatively value relevant only for large firms (informing investors on whether the research expenditure indicates expenses on unsuccessful projects that will not assure future benefits to firms). |

(continued)

Table 4.1. (cont.)

| Paper | Assets | Selection | Topics | Main conclusions |
|---|---|---|---|---|
| Oliveira et al. (2010) | Goodwill and intangible assets | 354 firm-year observations Portugal 1998–2008 | Intangible assets are value relevant. Value relevance of book value, earnings and recognised intangible assets under IFRS differs from value relevance of accounting information under Portuguese GAAP. | Intangible assets are associated with stock price. IFRS adoption had no impact on the value relevance of identifiable intangibles and a positive effect on the value relevance of goodwill. Value relevance of earnings has weakened after 2005, once accounting policy changed. |
| Lourenço and Curto (2008) | Investment property | 224 firms European countries 2005–2007 | Cost, fair value and disclosed fair value of investment property are priced differently by investors. Fair value of investment property in France, Germany, Sweden and the United Kingdom are priced by investors differently from each other. | Investors differentiate cost and fair value and disclosed fair value of investment property. Investors do not differentiate valuation implications of fair value in Germany, the United Kingdom (Continental and Anglo-Saxon models, respectively), France and Sweden (countries with medium level of shareholder protection). |
| Barth and Clinch (1998) | Tangible and intangible assets | 250 firms Australia 1991–1995 | Relevance, reliability, and timeliness of Australian asset revaluations differ: Across different types of assets. If revaluation is determined by the firm's director or an independent appraiser. According the age of the revalued amount. | Upward and downward revalued tangible and intangible assets are value relevant. Little evidence supports director-based revalued amounts being less relevant than independent appraiser-based revalued amounts. Timeliness is not sensitive to long-term asset revaluations. |

## Theoretical background

This research explores the value relevance of recognised biological assets under the theory of asymmetric information (Glaum *et al.*, 2013; Hitz, 2007; Healy and Papelu, 2001), which assures a strong background for the valuation purpose of financial reporting. Trustworthy and opportune information decreases the risk of valuation calculated by investors and enhances decision-making assessment (Glaum *et al.*, 2013). Therefore, measurement contributes to the decision-usefulness objective (Hitz, 2007) and additionally, disclosure mitigates information asymmetries in capital markets and reduces the cost of capital (Glaum *et al.*, 2013; Healy and Palepu, 2001). Nonetheless, financial statements are not effective in decreasing information asymmetries, if financial reporting is tendentiously partial and not complete (Glaum *et al.*, 2013).

### Key research issues

The first key research issue to examine is the ability of biological assets to explain market equity values. Where decision-usefulness is concerned, measurement plays an important role (Hitz, 2007) as timely information mitigates the risk of investors' valuation (Glaum *et al.*, 2013).

Although there are studies that confirm accounting information related to biological assets has an impact on investors' decision-making (Argilés Bosh *et al.*, 2012; Argilés *et al.*, 2011), there are other studies that do not support value relevance in the biological assets domain (Martins *et al.*, 2012). On the one hand, given the informational point of view, the replacement of historical cost to fair value in the measurement of such assets was favourable to the market, since the difference between the estimated market at fair value and accounting numbers was lower compared to measurement at historical cost. On the other hand, it seems that investors do not take into account this information in isolation when making decisions about their investments. Moreover, often fair value of biological assets is calculated on the basis of estimates, mainly through the discounted future cash flow. Therefore, measurement becomes more difficult to understand and may be less relevant to accounting information users.

Finally, in spite of the literature that supports value relevance regarding other non-financial assets, there is no strong expectation that biological assets are able to explain market equity values because of mixed empirical evidence in prior literature concerning biological assets. In other words, it seems that the literature does not support biological assets at fair value being value relevant under IAS 41.

The second key research issue embraces disclosure in the context of fair value relevance, in order to explore investors' perception of the incorporation of more information into financial statements. Firstly, it is essential to distinguish recognition from disclosure (Kun, 2013; Ahmed *et al.*, 2006; Ball, 2006; Davis-Friday *et al.*, 1999). Additionally, "the question as to whether amounts disclosed in the notes of the financial statements and those recognised on the face of the financial statements have a similar impact on share prices is an important one for accounting regulators, accounts preparers and auditors" (Al Jifri and Citron, 2009:137).

Given IASB's conceptual framework, disclosure is not a substitute for recognition. In order to be recognised, an item must have "a cost or value that can be measured with reliability" (paragraph no. 4.38.b, IASB Conceptual Framework). The same criteria are not applied for disclosed items. In this sense, and by analogy to the Financial Accounting Standards Board (FASB), investors distinguish recognised items as more reliable than disclosed items (Fried, 2012). Nonetheless, Choudhary (2011) and Holthausen and Watts (2001) support the idea that recognition suggests less reliability, since managers are more encouraged to manipulate recognised items than disclosed items. There are also other arguments that support the difference between the two, such as investors incorrectly underestimating disclosed items through a lack of expertise or due to the cost of processing information (Kun, 2013; Al Jifri and Citron, 2009). Conversely, the efficient market hypothesis suggests that recognition enhances slightly when the disclosure notes address the investors' information (Barth *et al.*, 2003).

To this extent, the current and controversial discussion justifies the introduction of the disclosure level effect in the present study. There is also the purpose of exceeding previous value relevance studies that deal only with recognition of biological assets (Huffman, 2013). Regarding other non-financial assets, such as human capital, and in line with the United States based studies, Samudhram *et al.* (2014) concluded that voluntarily disclosed employee costs in annual reports of listed firms are value relevant in Malaysia. However, such information should be analysed with caution, as it could suggest an alternative for managers to exercise discretionary behaviour with respect to disclosed human capital (Samudhram *et al.,* 2014). According to Tsalavoutas and Dionysiou (2014), a higher voluntary disclosure level supports positive valuation implications. Nonetheless, prior literature does not indicate any sign of there being a relationship between mandatory disclosure compliance and market valuation. For example, Leuz and Wysocki (2008:17) explain that "disclosure requirements specify which information a firm has to provide and force it to reveal this information in both good and bad times".

Referring to biological assets, as mentioned before, PwC (2011 and 2009) also advise firms to perform some voluntary disclosure of biological assets as an improvement to mandatory disclosure. In terms of the timber section, the PwC (2011 and 2009) concluded that firms have different levels of transparency concerning biological assets disclosure, and in certain cases there is a chance for further enhancement without discussing fair valuation assumptions. Moreover, taking into account the empirical evidence of the survey developed by Elad and Herbohn (2011), there is a lack of comparability between disclosure practices in which French firms tend to disclose less information on biological assets than firms from Australia and the United Kingdom. Given this diversified behaviour regarding the disclosure level of biological assets, a different impact on market valuation can be predicted. Additionally, regarding other non-financial assets, Baboukardos and Rimmel (2014) support the value relevance of goodwill only in firms with a high disclosure level. In this sense, there is a strong expectation that the value relevance of biological assets is higher in listed firms with a high disclosure level on biological assets.

# 5 Empirical evidence

## Questions

Based on previous considerations regarding accounting for biological assets under IAS 41, this chapter covers empirical evidence worldwide. Therefore, it embraces two main goals and the corresponding research questions.

The first objective aims to identify the firm and country-level drivers that could explain mandatory and voluntary disclosure and measurement practices of biological assets under IAS 41 with the following research questions:

(i) What is the disclosure level on biological assets in listed firms under IAS 41?
(ii) What firm and country-level drivers explain the differences in the disclosure level on biological assets among listed firms?
(iii) What firm and country-level drivers explain the differences in practices used to measure biological assets among listed firms?

The second objective aims to examine the value relevance of fair value of biological assets under IAS 41 in order to investigate the market valuation implications of this standard. Therefore, the following research questions are considered in this research:

(i) Are biological assets at fair value value relevant under IAS 41?
(ii) Is there a difference in the value relevance of biological assets between listed firms with high and low disclosure levels on biological assets?

**Sample**

This book explores a selection of listed firms worldwide that comply with the criteria of having first adopted IFRS before 2012. Throughout the research, data was collected in DataStream[1] and the chosen year was the most recent year with more up-to-date information in order to assure the maximum possible number of countries and consequently number of firms, as well as to provide research with recent data.

This research embraces three periods corresponding to both research goals: 2011, to examine disclosure practices; 2012, to study measurement practices; and a three-year period from 2011 to 2013, to explore the value relevance of biological assets under IAS 41. IFRS 1 – First-time adoption of IFRS allows for some exemptions and exceptions which may cause some constraints when analysing and making inferences about the information of the year of adoption (Callao Gastón *et al.*, 2010). Consequently, 2010 should be the limit year for considering firms that adopted IFRS (or equivalent standards), for examining disclosure practices and for exploring the value relevance of biological assets under IAS 41. In addition, 2011 should be the limit year for considering firms that adopted IFRS (or equivalent standards) to study measurement practices. In 2014, a project was already ongoing to change this standard where bearer biological assets (plants) are concerned. If this book considered data from 2014, biased results could be obtained as the firms had already been informed about the proposed amendments and that could influence their behaviour.

Initially, countries were selected that adopted IFRS until 2010 and 2011. For both years the selected countries are: Australia, Austria, Belgium, Bermuda, Brazil, Cayman Islands, Chile, China, Croatia, Cyprus, Denmark, Egypt, Faroe Islands, Finland, France, Germany, Greece, Hong Kong, Ireland, Italy, Kenya, Kuwait, Latvia, Lithuania, Luxembourg, Mauritius, Netherlands, New Zealand, Norway, Oman, Papua New Guinea, Peru, Philippines, Portugal, Russian Federation, South Africa, Spain, Sweden, Ukraine, United Arab Emirates and the United Kingdom. Additionally, Canada, South Korea and Poland are the selected countries for periods beginning in 2011.

Considering the corresponding selection of countries, firms that have biological assets were selected. The criterion was to follow one of the biological asset variables, all available in DataStream: biological assets – net book value, biological assets – gross and biological assets – current. When any of the drivers' proxies of the present study was not available in DataStream, there was an effort to obtain information in firms' annual reports to mitigate the effect of missing information.

## Disclosure index

The index is built based on the disclosures required by IAS 41 and calculated with the notes of the consolidated financial statements included in 2011, 2012 and 2013 annual report of this selection of firms.[2] It includes three categories: mandatory items, non-mandatory but recommended items, and non-mandatory, non-recommended items. The first and the second classifications cover all disclosure items required by IAS 41. The last category concerns voluntary information indicating that firms have exceeded IAS 41 disclosure requirements. Given the intrinsic complexity of biological assets fair valuation, non-mandatory, non-recommended items are only applicable to firms that measure biological assets at fair value. This third classification is constructed according to PwC (2011). Three topics are identified as being followed by their clients in disclosure practices, where the timber sector is concerned, namely: revealing the complexity of various parameters regarding the effect on the valuation; providing more information on the effects of variations in key factors; exposing assumptions on future prices and costs, as well as disclosing a sensitivity analysis with multiple parameters.

The disclosure index is adopted in this book for two research topics, namely: to analyse the disclosure level on biological assets in listed firms under IAS 41 and to test whether there is a difference in the value relevance of biological assets between listed firms with high and low disclosure levels on biological assets. The items selected for inclusion in the disclosure index and the results are shown in Appendix A.

Based on the literature about this research topic (Santos *et al.*, 2013; Lopes and Rodrigues, 2007; Owusu-Ansah, 1998), the disclosure index is dichotomous, unweighted and adjusted for non-applicable items. Firstly, a score of 1 is assigned to an item if it is disclosed, and a score of 0 otherwise, which means that the index is dichotomous. The maximum number of items is 40 or 27.[3] Secondly, each item is equally important for all three categories. Although a weighted index permits some dissimilarities, given the relative importance of certain items of information (Inchausti, 1997), here the assumption is that an unweighted approach will result in a minor bias, because the effort of the index is parallel in all three categories. Finally, the index follows a tolerant criterion (Santos *et al.*, 2013) and covers the applicability of any item to each firm. It excludes items where there is no information in the notes of the consolidated financial statements about one disclosure item of IAS 41. In this sense, adopting an adjusted index neglects the effect if the selected firms measure biological assets at fair value or at historical cost. There is only one exemption regarding the last attribute, such as the following item of IAS 41 [IAS 41.49]: "financial risk management strategies related to agricultural activity". Risk strategy related to biological assets is highly important in the sense that a firm is required to declare the overall strategy in the annual report. Therefore, if this item contains no information it is considered in the index as a non-disclosed item. The total score of the mandatory and voluntary disclosure index for biological assets (Index) in a firm is:

$$Index_i = \frac{\sum_{i=1}^{m} d_i}{m} \tag{1}$$

where $d_i = 0$ or 1, as follows: $d_i = 1$ if the item is disclosed and $d_i = 0$, otherwise; $m$ = maximum number of applicable items a firm may disclose.

Finally, the index follows two criteria, namely, reliability and validity, which are supported by Marston and Shrives (1991). It is reliable in the sense that the results can be replicated by another researcher and it is valid in the sense that it serves the purpose of the research.

## Main results

### Disclosure

#### Sample

The sample corresponds to 270 firms from 40 countries and 8 different sectors. The annual report of each firm, in particular, and the notes of the consolidated financial statements were analysed in order to calculate the disclosure index.

#### Firm and country-level drivers

Based on the previously mentioned current debate, biological assets intensity (BIO), ownership concentration (HELD), firm size (SIZE), auditor type (AUDIT), internationalisation level (INT), listing status (STOCK), profitability (ROE) and sector (SECTOR) are the chosen firm-level drivers to analyse disclosure of biological assets. The country-level driver is measured by legal status according to the following three classifications: the dichotomy of common law versus code law country (LEGAL); Leuz's cluster classification (CLUSTER); and the audit and enforcement classification by Brown *et al.* (2014) (AUD08, ENF08 and

AUD08_ENF08). In order to measure the disclosure level, this research applies the disclosure index, which is constructed and calculated as previously explained. The proxies for measuring such drivers, the variable codes of DataStream and the expected signals to infer the impact on the disclosure level are included in Appendix B.

*Some descriptive evidence*

Appendix C presents the descriptive statistics for the variables employed in the study. There is a wide range in the disclosure index scores in the selection: the highest disclosure score obtained is 100 by the firm Holmen (Sweden) and the lowest is 0 by the following firms: Donegal (Ireland), Kuwait Food Company (Kuwait), L.D.C. (France) and Randon (Brazil). Table 5.1 presents the 10 selected firms that have higher and lower disclosure levels with the corresponding country and sector.

Regarding the disclosure level, the number of firms that disclose biological assets information, by disclosure item, is summarised in Appendix A. The most frequently reported items are: "Reconciliation of changes in the carrying amount of biological assets between the beginning and the end of the period" (n=248; [IAS 41.50]); "This reconciliation includes desegregation" (n=242; [IAS 41.50]); and "Description of each group of biological assets" (n=230; [IAS 41.41]). This evidence is consistent with prior literature (Silva *et al.*, 2012) for Brazilian firms. The least reported items are: "Range of estimates within which fair value is highly likely to lie" (n=2; [IAS 41.54]), when the entity measures biological assets at their cost less any accumulated depreciation and any accumulated impairment losses; and "Unfulfilled conditions and other contingencies attaching to government grants" (n=1; [IAS 41.57]). Overall, these findings suggest that there is an opportunity for improving biological assets disclosure, as concluded by PwC (2011) for the timber sector. Additionally, Table 5.2 presents the ranking of the most representative countries by the number of firms and their average disclosure level.[4] For example, Australia corresponds to 25 firms and a level of 63.00 and Hong Kong corresponds to 24 firms and a level of 67.00.

Finally, it is commonly established that correlations between independent variables are not risky in multivariate analysis unless they exceed 0.80 or 0.90 (Gujarati, 1995). Appendix E reveals no highly correlated independent variables, given Pearson's correlation; therefore, all variables are maintained in the model. For example, the disclosure index is positively correlated to biological assets intensity at a 1% level of significance.

*Table 5.1.* Ten firms with higher and lower disclosure levels by country and sector

*Higher disclosure level*

| Firm | Country | Sector | Index |
|---|---|---|---|
| Holmen | Sweden | Manufacturing | 1.00 |
| Forestal Cholguan | Chile | Manufacturing | 0.95 |
| Vipingo Plantations | Kenya | Agriculture, forestry, fishing and mining | 0.95 |
| Distell Group | South Africa | Manufacturing | 0.94 |
| Vina San Pedro | Chile | Manufacturing | 0.94 |
| R.E.A. Holdings PLC | United Kingdom | Agriculture, forestry, fishing and mining | 0.90 |
| Select Harvests | Australia | Manufacturing | 0.89 |
| York Timber | South Africa | Manufacturing | 0.89 |
| Stolt Nielsen | United Kingdom | Transportation and pub. utilities | 0.89 |
| Livestock Imp. Corporation | New Zealand | Agriculture, forestry, fishing and mining | 0.88 |

*Lower disclosure level*

| Firm | Country | Sector | Index |
|---|---|---|---|
| Donegal | Ireland | Manufacturing | 0.00 |
| Kuwait Food Company | Kuwait | Retail trade | 0.00 |
| L.D.C. | France | Manufacturing | 0.00 |
| Randon | Brazil | Manufacturing | 0.00 |
| Siguldas | Latvia | Agriculture, forestry, fishing and mining | 0.07 |
| Unilever | Netherlands | Manufacturing | 0.09 |
| Pernod Ricard | France | Manufacturing | 0.13 |
| BTG PLC | United Kingdom | Manufacturing | 0.13 |
| Vealls Limited | Australia | Services | 0.17 |
| Carbon Conscious | Australia | Transportation and pub. utilities | 0.17 |

*Table 5.2.* Ranking of the more representative countries by the number of firms and their average disclosure level

| Country | Disclosure | |
|---|---|---|
| | Number of firms | Disclosure index |
| | | 2011 |
| Chile | 30 | 52.00 |
| Brazil | 28 | 59.00 |
| Australia | 25 | 63.00 |
| Hong Kong | 24 | 67.00 |
| South Africa | 20 | 49.00 |
| United Kingdom | 17 | 60.00 |
| China | 11 | 44.00 |
| New Zealand | 11 | 64.00 |
| France | 9 | 52.00 |
| Norway | 9 | 47.00 |
| Others | 86 | – |
| Total | **270** | – |

*Explanatory drivers*

This study adopts an ordinary least squares (OLS) regression model with the following equations:

$$
\begin{aligned}
Index_i = {} & b_0 + b_1 BIO + b_2 HELD + b_3 SIZE + b_4 AUDIT \\
& + b_5 INT + b_6 STOCK + b_7 ROE + \\
& + b_8 \sum_{j=1}^{j=3} SECTOR_j + b_9 LEGAL + u_i
\end{aligned}
\tag{2}
$$

$$
\begin{aligned}
Index_i = {} & b_0 + b_1 BIO + b_2 HELD + b_3 SIZE \\
& + b_4 AUDIT + b_5 INT + b_6 STOCK + b_7 ROE + \\
& + b_8 \sum_{j=1}^{j=3} SECTOR_j + b_9 \sum_{l=1}^{l=3} CLUSTER_l + u_i
\end{aligned}
\tag{3}
$$

In both regressions, the presence of heteroscedasticity is analysed with White's general test (White, 1980). This test indicates the presence of heteroscedasticity in all regressions; as a result, both equations are re-estimated, adjusting the standard errors for heteroscedasticity. Table 5.3 presents the disclosure drivers' behaviour.

The results are provided in Appendix F. The feasibility of the regression model is given by the adjusted R-squared value that increases from equation (2) to equation (3). Regarding firm-level drivers, the effective

*Table 5.3.* Disclosure drivers' behaviour

| Proxies | Variables code | Expected signals | Effective signals |
|---|---|---|---|
| Biological assets intensity | BIO | Positive | Positive |
| Ownership concentration | HELD | Negative | Positive |
| Firm size | SIZE | Positive | Positive |
| Auditor type | AUDIT | Positive | n/a |
| Internationalisation level | INT | Positive | n/a |
| Listing status | STOCK | Positive | n/a |
| Profitability | ROE | No expected signal | n/a |
| Sector | SECTOR | Positive | Positive |
| Legal status | LEGAL | Positive | Positive |
| | CLUSTER | Positive | Positive |
| | AUD08 | Positive | Negative |
| | ENF08 | Positive | n/a |
| | AUD08_ENF08 | Positive | Negative |

signal of biological assets intensity is consistent with Scherch *et al.* (2013) and also with other non-financial assets, for example goodwill impairment (Amiraslani *et al.*, 2013; Glaum *et al.* 2013; Heitzman *et al.*, 2010; Shalev, 2009).

Surprisingly, ownership concentration is supported by the model but exhibits a positive signal. Rahman *et al.* (2002) compared accounting regulations and accounting practices in Australia and New Zealand and revealed that although ownership concentration does not seem to be related to mandatory disclosure, it exhibits a positive sign related to voluntary disclosure.

Concerning firm size, this finding is consistent with prior literature (Amiraslani *et al.*, 2013; Glaum *et al.*, 2013; Lan *et al.*, 2013; Oliveira *et al.*, 2006; Depoers, 2000). When it comes to sector (on average and other parameters being equal), firms in sector 1 (agriculture, forestry, fishing and mining) and sector 2 (manufacturing) exhibit a disclosure level which is higher than the disclosure level of firms that belong to other sectors. This finding is consistent with the fact that these sectors are associated with biological assets.

Furthermore, the type of auditor, internationalisation level, listing status and profitability are not supported by the results. Regarding the type of auditor, this result is probably related to the fact that the majority of the firms are audited by a Big 4 auditing firm and so the variable has little explanatory power. Regarding the negative sign, Lan *et al.* (2013) analysed the voluntary disclosure drivers of Chinese listed firms and suggested that, most likely, firms audited by the Big 4 auditing firms were paid more attention than other firms and tended to disclose more information through other means, such as the media. Also, regarding biological assets disclosure, Elad and Herbohn (2011:116) concluded that:

> notwithstanding this low level of compliance none of the companies received a qualified audit opinion due to insufficient disclosure. Presumably, the auditors adopted a flexible approach that recognises the salience of each item and the individual circumstances of each company when assessing the adequacy of disclosure.

With regard to the internationalisation level, Oliveira *et al.* (2006) also rejected the extent of voluntary disclosure of intangible information being positively related to the internationalisation of the firm, which was measured by the same variable. In terms of the listing status, Amiraslani *et al.* (2013) state that this variable is not considered a significant determinant of compliance with goodwill impairment disclosure. Finally, considering profitability, Chavent *et al.* (2006) investigated the 2011 annual report of 100 French firms that integrate the *Société des Bourses Françaises* (SBF) 120 stock index and found that the disclosure pattern is not associated with return on equity.

Considering the country-level driver, both the common law versus code law country classification, supported by La Porta *et al.* (1998), and a cluster classification that represents a more recent perspective introduced by Leuz (2010) are in accordance with the theoretical background. Firms that belong to common law countries or to outsider economies improve the extent of mandatory and voluntary disclosure of biological assets.

Surprisingly, with regard to the audit and enforcement classification by Brown *et al.* (2014), the results show that mandatory and voluntary disclosure is statistically negatively related to audit proxy in equation (4) and the results do not support the variable enforcement in equation (5). When both measures are taken together (audit and enforcement), the results corroborate the major negative influence of audit measure in equation (6). However, the adjusted R-squared value confirms that including the audit and enforcement proxies separately or together, the explanatory power of the model is improved when compared to legal proxy and cluster proxy of earlier research.

$$Index_i = b_0 + b_1 BIO + b_2 HELD + b_3 SIZE$$
$$+ b_4 AUDIT + b_5 INT + b_6 STOCK + b_7 ROE +$$
$$+ b_8 \sum\nolimits_{j=1}^{j=4} SECTOR_j + b_9 AUD08 + u_i \qquad (4)$$

$$Index_i = b_0 + b_1 BIO + b_2 HELD + b_3 SIZE$$
$$+ b_4 AUDIT + b_5 INT + b_6 STOCK + b_7 ROE +$$
$$+ b_8 \sum\nolimits_{j=1}^{j=4} SECTOR_j + b_9 ENF08 + u_i \qquad (5)$$

$$Index_i = b_0 + b_1 BIO + b_2 HELD + b_3 SIZE$$
$$+ b_4 AUDIT + b_5 INT + b_6 STOCK + b_7 ROE +$$
$$+ b_8 \sum\nolimits_{j=1}^{j=4} SECTOR_j + b_9 AUD08\_ENF08 + u_i \qquad (6)$$

In order to understand these results, audit proxy, in a certain way, corroborates the negative sign for the firm-level driver – auditor type (the firm is audited by a Big 4 auditing firm) although this variable exhibits no statistical significance. Even though there are several advantages related to those measures, as previously documented, Preiato *et al.* (2015) suggest some possible limitations. The audit proxy mostly represents input measures and there is little variation between countries for several of them. Taking enforcement proxy into account, there is also a great variation in the extent of enforcement activities among the countries where enforcement action is taken. Moreover, the scoring method of Brown *et al.* (2014) does not measure that variation precisely. There is also no evidence of the relationship of the items included in the index. This approach excludes measures of the frequency of professional disciplinary action taken against accountants and auditors and its influence on audit practice. Consequently, the particular behaviour of biological assets and some constraints associated with audit and enforcement proxies could be probable explanations of these results.

*Conclusions*

With regard to the disclosure level by listed firms on biological assets under IAS 41, evidence shows that the corresponding index stands in a wide range of values, although the majority of disclosure items are mandatory. Results indicate that 1) firms highly disclose the reconciliation of changes of biological assets between the beginning and the end of the period with desegregation and 2) tend to ignore the requirement of disclosing the range of estimates of fair value applied to biological assets measurement.

With respect to mandatory and voluntary disclosure of biological assets, firm-level drivers, such as biological assets intensity, firm size and belonging to agricultural and manufacturing sectors, have a significant positive impact on mandatory and voluntary disclosure practices. Unexpectedly, ownership concentration also has a significant positive impact on mandatory and voluntary disclosure practices. Bearing in mind country-level drivers, firms that belong to common law countries or to outsider economies improve the extent of mandatory and voluntary disclosure of biological assets. Surprisingly, the results show that mandatory and voluntary disclosure is statistically negatively related to audit proxy or to audit and enforcement proxy, when considered together, and the results do not support the variable enforcement. Although several studies have already adopted the audit and enforcement proxies suggested by Brown *et al.* (2014), this index has some possible limitations, as previously explained. In addition, the sample is small and biological assets represent a specific segment of the study. Could it be a constraint of IAS 41 per se, since the level of disclosure is also low?

Overall, two main findings corroborate previous studies: the need to improve the disclosure level and the dichotomy of common law versus code law countries regarding this research topic.

### *Measurement*

#### *Sample*

The sample corresponds to 324 firms from 33 countries and 8 different sectors. The annual report of each firm was analysed to identify the measurement practice (fair value or historical cost) of the biological assets represented in the consolidated financial statements (in particular, in the corresponding notes). Table 5.4 presents the distribution of the more representative number of firms by country with the related measurement practice.[5]

#### *Relationship between measurement practice and the type of biological assets*

Before explaining the firm and country-level drivers and in order to bring awareness to the selected firms of this study and ascertain any particular behaviour, the relationship between the measurement practice (fair

*Table 5.4.* Number of firms by country with the related measurement practice

| Nation | Historical cost | Fair value | Total |
|---|---|---|---|
| Australia | 1 | 20 | 21 |
| Brazil | 7 | 22 | 29 |
| Chile | 11 | 15 | 26 |
| China | 54 | 13 | 67 |
| Hong Kong | 1 | 25 | 26 |
| Korea (South) | 14 | 4 | 18 |
| New Zealand | - | 10 | 10 |
| South Africa | - | 18 | 18 |
| Sweden | - | 9 | 9 |
| United Kingdom | - | 19 | 19 |
| Others | 16 | 65 | 81 |
| Total | **104** | **220** | **324** |

value or historical cost) and the type of biological assets was tested with the chi-squared test (Greene, 2012). According to IAS 41, biological assets could be divided into bearer biological assets and consumable biological assets. Based on the 2012 annual reports of the selected 324 listed firms, it was possible to identify the type of biological assets in each firm.

Given the chi-squared test results presented in Appendix G, overall, biological assets and the measurement policy adopted by firms are related. Therefore, based on the previous classification, namely, bearer biological assets and consumable biological assets, the selection was split and submitted under the same approach. The results suggest that although consumable biological assets and their measurement policy are also related, the same does not apply to bearer biological assets. In this case, both variables are independent. Since the bearer biological assets are more complex to measure due to the lack of active markets, this absence of relationship could lead to a higher propensity to follow the unreliability clause of fair value or even cause higher discretionary behaviour of managers. Consequently, it seems that there are other reasons that could support the measurement practices of bearer biological assets.

*Firm and country-level drivers*

Based on the current debate, biological assets intensity, firm size, regulation expertise, potential growth, leverage and sector are the chosen firm-level drivers for analysing the measurement of biological assets. The country-level driver is measured by legal status according to regulatory quality: a worldwide governance indicator supported by Kaufmann *et al.* (2011). The proxies for measuring such drivers, the variable codes of DataStream and the expected signals to infer the impact on the measurement practice are included in Appendix B.

*Some descriptive evidence*

Appendix C presents the descriptive statistics for the variables employed in the study. There is a wide range of biological assets intensity (BIO) in the selection, taking into account that this variable corresponds to the ratio between biological assets and total assets: the observed maximum is 92.60 and the minimum is excessively close to zero. The majority of selected firms (87.04%) correspond to firms that are not listed on any foreign stock exchange (STOCK), and 63.83% of them measure biological assets at fair value. Taking sector into consideration, 28.39% of selected firms relates to agriculture, forestry, fishing and mining, and 78.26% of them measure biological assets at fair value.

Appendix E reveals no highly correlated independent variables, given Pearson's correlation; therefore, all variables are maintained in the model. For example, at 1% level of significance, biological assets intensity is positively correlated to the legal status variable and negatively correlated to the potential growth variable.

*Explanatory drivers*

This research considers a logit regression model. The following equations include a binary dependent variable (FAIR) that corresponds to the measurement practice (1, if the firm measures biological assets at fair value; 0, if the firm measures biological assets at historical cost), and explores several drivers that are expected to be related to the measurement of biological assets.

$$
\begin{aligned}
Fair = b_0 &+ b_1 BIO + b_2 SIZE + b_3 STOCK + b_4 IFRS \\
&+ b_5 GROWTH + b_6 LEV + b_7 \Sigma^{j=1,2,3} SECTOR_j + \qquad (7) \\
&+ b_8 QUALITY + u_i
\end{aligned}
$$

The presence of heteroscedasticity is analysed with Huber and White's general test (White, 1980). Table 5.5 presents the measurement drivers' behaviour.

The results are provided in Appendix I. All variables are statistically and positively significant with two exceptions. The leverage variable (LEV) is not statistically significant and potential growth (GROWTH)

*Table 5.5.* Measurement drivers' behaviour

| Proxies | Variables code | Expected signals | Effective signals |
|---|---|---|---|
| Biological assets intensity | BIO | Positive | Positive |
| Firm size | SIZE | No expected signal | Positive |
| Listing status | STOCK | Positive | Positive |
| Regulation expertise | IFRS | Positive | Positive |
| Potential growth | GROWTH | Positive | n/a |
| Leverage | LEV | Positive | n/a |
| Sector | SECTOR | Positive | Positive |
| Legal status | QUALITY | Positive | Positive |

is statistically significant, but it has a negative coefficient, meaning that the more the ratio between market value to book value increased, the lower the logit for fair value measurement for biological assets.

Given the transformation of regression coefficients (odds ratio), this study interprets the effect that independent variables have on the probability of fair value measurement for biological assets.

For dummy independent variables, results are as follows: since listing status (STOCK) denotes 1 whether the firm is listed on one foreign stock exchange or is multi-listed, or 0 otherwise, an odds ratio equal to 15.370 estimates that fair value measurement for biological assets is more than 15 times as likely to occur among firms that are listed on one foreign stock exchange or are multi-listed than the other selected firms. This finding is consistent with Daniel *et al.* (2010) regarding non-financial assets, and with Taplin *et al.* (2014) in terms of investment property.

Additionally, for sector (SECTOR), the corresponding odds ratio equal to 1.914 estimates that fair value measurement for biological assets is more than 1.9 times as likely to occur among firms that belong to the agriculture, forestry, fishing, mining and manufacturing sectors than firms that belong to other sectors. Similar to this finding, Demaria and Dufour (2007) confirm that the financial sector is linked to IFRS choices in the French context.

For continuous variables, starting with firm size (SIZE), the odds ratio is 1.698. Thus, for each unit increase in the logarithm of total assets (expressed in EUR'000) the odds of choosing fair value increases by 69.80%. In this case, in order to interpret the odds ratio (because the variable is expressed in logarithm form), it is possible to explain the specific effect of a unit increasing in firm size considering the range of the variables in the study selection. For instance, an increase in firm size from 5 to 6 (expressed in logarithm of total assets) means that an increase of $(e^6 - e^5)$ x 1.000=255.016 euros increases the odds of choosing fair value by 69.80%. These results are also supported by Cairns *et al.* (2011) for biological assets.

For other continuous variables, one unit variation in each variable does not clearly explain the impact on fair value choice. Therefore, the odds ratio was transformed taking into consideration a change of 0.10 (10%).

Biological assets intensity (BIO) varies widely between almost 0 and 92.60. The odds ratio was transformed at $e^{0.079}$ =1.082, taking into consideration a change of 0.10 (10%) in the variable instead of a unit change. Because $e^{0.079/10} = 1.008$, this means that the odds of choosing fair value for biological assets are multiplied by 1.008 for each additional 10% variation in BIO. Hence, for each 10% increase in this variable, there is a 0.8% increase in the odds of fair value choice. This finding is consistent with Daniel *et al.* (2010) regarding non-financial assets, and with Christensen and Nikolaev (2013) and Hlaing and Pourjalali (2012) in terms of investment property.

The regulation expertise (IFRS) ranges from 0.30 to 1.04. Again, instead of considering the odds ratio at 19.735 ($e^{2.982}$), it is interpreted as $e^{2.982/10} = 1.347$. For each 10% increase in regulation expertise, there is a 35% increase in the odds of fair value choice. This finding is consistent with Daniel *et al.* (2010) regarding non-financial assets.

Potential growth (GROWTH) ranges from –3.28 to 16.35 in the study selection. In order to calculate the impact on the fair value choice, the odds ratio $e^{-0.217} = 0.805$ was transformed, taking into consideration a change of 0.10 (10%) in the variable instead of a unit change. In this case, $e^{-0.217/10} = 0.978$ means that the odds of choosing fair value for biological assets is multiplied by 0.98 for each additional 10% variation in GROWTH. In other words, the odds of choosing fair value are reduced by $(1–0.98) \times 100 = 2\%$ for each 10% increase in potential growth. Missonier-Piera (2007) also concluded that fixed-asset revaluation in Switzerland is negatively influenced by growth opportunities.

The legal status (QUALITY) varies between –0.26 to 1.94. Because the odds ratio is equal to 3.911 ($e^{1.364}$), it is interpreted as $e^{1.364/10} = 1.146$. For each 10% increase in regulatory quality, there is a 15% increase in the odds of fair value choice.

Finally, the results show that there is no relationship with the leverage variable (LEV). Regarding investment property, Taplin *et al.* (2014) found insignificant evidence to support leverage. Also, Demaria and

Dufour (2007) confirm that leverage is not linked to IFRS choices in the French context.

Taking into account that regulation expertise (IFRS) is statistically and positively significant at less than 0.01, the study introduced the combination between this variable and the sector (SECTOR), improving the effect of the firms with higher regulation expertise that belong to the following sectors: agriculture, forestry, fishing, mining and manufacturing.

In this sense, the model includes an additional variable in equation (8) and the results are provided in Appendix I. The new variable is also statistically and positively significant and increases the feasibility of the regression model improving the McFadden R-squared measure.

$$
\begin{aligned}
Fair = {} & b_0 + b_1 BIO + b_2 SIZE + b_3\, STOCK + b_4\, IFRS \\
& + b_5 GROWTH + b_6 LEV + b_7 IFRS \times \textstyle\sum^{\,j=1,2,3} SECTOR_j \quad (8) \\
& + b_8 QUALITY + u_i
\end{aligned}
$$

In order to provide some robustness tests, two additional analyses were conducted. Firstly, Appendix J and Appendix K present, respectively, the correct prediction for the dependent variable and the Andrews and Hosmer–Lemeshow statistic to test the overall model (Hosmer *et al.*, 2013; Peng *et al.*, 2002; Stone and Rasp, 1991). According to Appendix J, the logit model correctly identifies 72% of firms that measure biological assets at historical cost (specificity) and 90% of firms that measure biological assets at fair value (sensitivity). In Appendix K, both Andrews and Hosmer–Lemeshow's statistics are statistically significant.

Secondly, given the results related to sector, firms that belong to the agriculture, forestry, fishing, mining and manufacturing sectors denote a higher probability to choose fair value for measuring their biological assets. With the purpose of assuring a more detailed analysis and ascertaining different behaviour according to sector, the model was re-estimated splitting the sectors. Appendix L shows that the agriculture, forestry, fishing and mining sectors are statistically and positively significant (odds ratio of 1.914, first test and 3.226, second test) and the manufacturing sector is statistically and negatively significant (odds ratio of 0.480, first test and 0.363, second test). Moreover, in order to identify which sub-sectors belong to the agriculture, forestry, fishing and mining sectors and to the manufacturing sector, which are responsible for these results, another analysis was performed. A two-digit sic-code division was considered according to agricultural and manufacturing sub-sectors that exhibit a higher number of firms to avoid any biased results, as presented in Table 5.6.

Regarding the agricultural sector, the model was re-estimated taking into consideration two sub-sectors: agricultural production – crops

*Table 5.6.* Selection distribution

| sic-code classification (two-digit) | Number of firms |
|---|---|
| 01 – Agricultural Production – Crops | 34 |
| 02 – Agricultural Production – Livestock and Animal Specialties | 27 |
| Others | 31 |
| **Agriculture, forestry and fishing and mining** | **92** |
| 20 – Food and Kindred Products (includes 29 firms in the sub-sector Beverages) | 98 |
| 26 – Paper and Allied Products | 27 |
| Others | 57 |
| **Manufacturing** | **182** |
| **Others** | **50** |
| **Total selection** | **324** |

(sic-code 01) and agricultural production – livestock and animal specialties (sic-code 02). When analysed individually, none of the sectors is statistically significant (odds ratio of 1.702, crops and 1.239, livestock and animal specialties).

Considering the manufacturing sector, the model was re-estimated taking two sub-sectors into account: paper and allied products (sic-code 26) and food and kindred products (sic-code 20). Although the paper and allied products sub-sector is not statistically significant (odds ratio of 0.912), the food and kindred products sub-sector is statistically and negatively significant (odds ratio of 0.367). Therefore, in order to assure a more bounded analysis, a three-digit sic-code division was considered and the beverages sub-sector was identified (sic-code 208) as being responsible for the negative results (odds ratio of 0.139). A plausible explanation could be the fact that this sub-sector represents the firms that have bearer biological assets, which are more complex to measure due to a lack of active markets; therefore, they have a higher propensity to follow the unreliability clause of fair value. Appendix M shows these findings.

Overall, only firms that belong to the agriculture, forestry, fishing and mining sectors denote a higher probability to choose fair value for measuring biological assets.

*Conclusions*

As previously mentioned, IAS 41 requires biological assets to be measured at fair value less costs to sell. Ideally, firms that measure biological assets at historical cost should correspond to firms with no conditions to report biological assets at fair value. This book builds on and also supports earlier studies that claim that there are other reasons related to firm and country environment that can explain the adoption of historical cost, even when the unreliability clause of fair value does not apply.

Firm-level drivers, biological assets intensity, firm size, being listed on one or more foreign stock exchange, regulation expertise and belonging to either the agricultural or manufacturing sectors all have a significant positive impact on the probability of fair value measurement for biological assets. Regarding sector, individually, agriculture and manufacturing exhibit a different behaviour. Firms that belong to the agricultural sector are more likely to use the fair value measurement model. Firms that belong to the manufacturing sector tend to choose, to a lesser extent, fair value to measure biological assets. In particular, the beverages sub-sector corresponds to firms that have bearer biological assets, which are more difficult to measure given the absence of active markets; consequently, they have a higher probability of avoiding fair value measurement. Finally, results corroborate country-level drivers in the sense that firms which belong to more developed countries, according to governance indicators (Kaufmann *et al.*, 2011), are more likely to use the fair value measurement model, avoiding the use of the unreliability clause of fair value.

### *Fair value relevance of biological assets*

#### *Sample*

This study includes panel data drawn from a selection of 389[6] firm-year observations of listed firms that had adopted IFRS until 2010, from 27 countries and 8 different sectors, between 2011 and 2013. The selection contains different amounts of both recognised biological assets in the face of financial statements and disclosed information in the notes of the consolidated financial statements only under fair value measurement. Therefore, firms under historical cost valuation were not considered.

#### *Research model*

Value relevance research examines the association between equity market values and accounting amounts. This book examines the value relevance of biological assets. Specifically, the accounting-based valuation model of Ohlson (1995) is adjusted to determine firm value. In general, this model represents firm value as a linear function of the book value of equity and earnings per share. With regard to biological assets, Martins *et al.* (2012) followed this methodology. They argue that this model can effectively measure the sensitivity, and cause and effect, between the book value and market value of a given firm. For non-financial assets (such as goodwill, investment property and tangible and intangible assets), this approach has been adopted by Baboukardos and Rimmel (2014), Oliveira *et al.* (2010), Lourenço and Curto (2008), and Barth and Clinch (1998). Additionally, this book also tests this valuation model by assessing the effects of disclosure levels, following Baboukardos and Rimmel (2014) and Al Jifri and Citron (2009).

Value relevance of recognised biological assets was tested in a regression where a firm's market value is a function of the book value of equity and earnings. This relation is tested in equation (9) with market value per share as the dependent variable (MV), and book value per share (BV) and earnings per share (E) as the independent variables. Moreover, all models include two control variables: firm size and industry sector.

$$MV_{it} = b_0 + b_1 BV_{it} + b_2 E_{it} + b_3 SIZE_{it} + b_4 \sum{}^{j=1,2,3} SECTOR_{jit} + u_{it} \quad (9)$$

In order to test the first research question, the book value of equity is then divided into two variables: the book value of equity excluding biological assets (BV-BA) and biological assets (BA). The coefficient $b_2$ assures a response to the value relevance of biological assets under IAS 41.

$$MV_{it} = b_0 + b_1 (BV\text{-}BA)_{it} + b_2 BA_{it} + b_3 E_{it} + b_4 SIZE_{it}$$
$$+ b_5 \sum{}^{j=1,2,3} SECTOR_{jit} + u_{it} \quad (10)$$

To test the second research question, the model below adds the effect of disclosure. The aim is to investigate whether there is a systematic difference in biological asset valuation effects between firms with relatively high and relatively low levels of disclosure of biological assets. The coefficient $b_5$ assures a response to the value relevance of biological assets regarding mandatory and voluntary disclosure. Dindex is a dummy variable based on whether the disclosure index for the biological assets of each firm is below the first quartile, in the middle quartiles, or in the fourth quartile of the sample's disclosure index distribution.

$$MV_{it} = b_0 + b_1 (BV\text{-}BA)_{it} + b_2 BA_{it} + b_3 E_{it} + b_4 \sum{}^{j=1,2,3} Dindex_{jit}$$
$$+ b_5 \sum{}^{j=1,2,3} Dindex_{jit} \times BA_{it} + b_6 SIZE_{it}$$
$$+ b_7 \sum{}^{j=1,2,3} SECTOR_{jit} + u_{it} \quad (11)$$

*Variables description*

The proxies and expected signals of the independent variables introduced above are described in Appendix B.[7] Data were collected in DataStream and in annual reports of firms between 2011 and 2013. Regarding the disclosure index, the maximum number of items is 27. According to Commission Regulation (EU) no. 1255/2012 of 11 December 2012, IFRS 13 is applied when another IFRS requires or permits fair value measurement or disclosures about fair value measurements. Consequently, this standard sets out amendments in several standards, such as in IAS 41, by deleting paragraphs 47 and 48. An entity shall apply amendments for annual periods beginning on or after 1 January 2013. As a result, the disclosure score, in particular for 2013, is 27 or 25, respectively. Items selected to be included in the disclosure index and results are shown in Appendix A.

*Some descriptive evidence*

Appendix C presents the descriptive statistics for the variables employed in the study. Regarding the disclosure level, the number of firms that disclose biological assets information, by disclosure item, is summarised in Appendix A. The most frequently reported items are the same as those obtained in the disclosure research topic: "A reconciliation of changes in the carrying amount of biological assets between the beginning and the end of the period" (n=368; [IAS 41.50]); "This reconciliation includes desegregation" (n=368; [IAS 41.50]). The least reported items are: "The aggregate gain or loss arising during the current period on initial recognition of agricultural produce" (n=9; [IAS 41.40]) and "The nature and extent of government grants recognised in the financial statements" (n=12; [IAS 41.57]). Table 5.7 presents the ranking of the more representative countries by the number of firms and their average disclosure level between 2011 and 2013.[8] Once more, the results show some discrepancy of information between firms and some lack of compliance regarding IAS 41.

Given the absence of disclosure, Tsalavoutas *et al.* (2014) suggest that firms should provide an explicit statement explaining when disclosure is not material or clarifying when disclosure is unreasonable on standard items. This would improve firm comparability and decrease information asymmetry across firms. Tsalavoutas *et al.* (2014) developed a recent report that discloses some recommendations for other non-financial assets. Based on a sample of 544 firms worldwide for the financial year 2010–2011, one goal of the study was to examine the

*Table 5.7.* Ranking of the more representative countries by the number of firms and their average disclosure level

| Country | Value relevance | | | |
| | Number of firms | Disclosure index | | |
| | | 2011 | 2012 | 2013 |
| --- | --- | --- | --- | --- |
| Chile | 10 | 59.00 | 59.00 | 61.00 |
| Brazil | 15 | 61.00 | 63.00 | 62.00 |
| Australia | 16 | 59.00 | 61.00 | 61.00 |
| Hong Kong | 22 | 57.00 | 57.00 | 60.00 |
| South Africa | 15 | 57.00 | 58.00 | 59.00 |
| United Kingdom | 8 | 76.00 | 76.00 | 75.00 |
| New Zealand | 6 | 63.00 | 63.00 | 65.00 |
| France | 4 | 45.00 | 48.00 | 47.00 |
| Norway | 5 | 58.00 | 58.00 | 62.00 |
| Philippines | 3 | 64.00 | 64.00 | 67.00 |
| Others | 28 | - | - | - |
| Total | **132** | - | - | - |

level of compliance with the mandated disclosures concerning mergers and acquisitions, intangibles and impairment assets. Overall, the report states that information between firms diverges considerably and that there is some level of non-compliance with regard to these three accounting issues. Firstly, the study recommends determining whether firms consider certain transactions not to be material enough, if the standards are not clear enough or if firms intentionally fail to follow the mandatory disclosure requirements. In this sense, preparers, auditors, regulators and enforcement bodies need to be focused on the improvement of the disclosure level by firms and on eliminating ambiguity in the interpretation of standards in order to assure greater comparability of the information provided by firms.

Appendix E presents Pearson's rank correlation coefficients. This set of correlations shows that all the independent variables are correlated positively with stock price. Regarding the first research question, the correlation coefficient of biological assets per share (BA) with market price per share (MV) is a preliminary signal that biological assets are value relevant on a univariate basis.

*Explanatory drivers*

This study adjusts the original accounting-based valuation model developed by Ohlson (Ohlson, 1995) from 2011 to 2013, by following the

*Table 5.8.* Value relevance drivers' behaviour

| Proxies | Variables code | Expected signals | Effective signals |
|---|---|---|---|
| Book value per share | BV | Positive | Positive |
| Biological assets per share | BA | No expected signal | Positive |
| Earnings per share | E | Positive | Positive |
| Disclosure index ranking | Dindex | Positive | Positive |
| Firm size | SIZE | Positive | Positive |
| Sector | SECTOR | Positive | n/a |

panel least squares method, given the three equations previously presented. Firstly, the data set was submitted to a random effects model (Greene, 2012). The Hausman test[9] was then applied and the results infer that a fixed effects model is the appropriate model for this sample. The presence of heteroskedasticity is taken into account with White diagonal standard errors and covariance (White, 1980). In order to reduce heteroskedasticity, all the variables (except control variables) are deflated by the number of common shares outstanding (Barth and Clinch, 2009). Table 5.8 presents the value relevance drivers' behaviour.

Appendix N shows estimated coefficients of the panel least square regressions for the three equations. In general, value relevance is tested in equation (9) with book value per share (BV) and earnings per share (E). The coefficient of biological assets per share (BA) assures the response to value relevance in both equations (10) and (11). Then, value relevance of biological assets regarding mandatory and voluntary disclosure is included in equation (11) and it is measured by the coefficient of the crossed variable between the disclosure index ranking (Dindex) and biological assets per share (BA). Overall, the adjusted R-squared value of the three equations indicates that introducing biological assets and the corresponding disclosure level separately improves, even slightly, the explanatory power of the model.

In general, book value per share and earnings per share are associated with firms' market value, given equation (9). In order to test the first research question, equation (10) excludes biological assets per share from book value per share. The results confirm that biological assets are value relevant at fair value under IAS 41.

Regarding the second research question, equation (11) tests whether there is a difference in the value relevance of biological assets between listed firms with high and low disclosure levels on biological assets. This regression includes the interaction variable between the dummy variable related to the disclosure level and biological assets per share. As a result, this evidence confirms the second research question, which states that value relevance of biological assets is higher in listed firms with high disclosure level on biological assets.

In order to provide an additional analysis and given the classification under IAS 41, namely bearer and consumable biological assets, the selection was divided. Equation (11) is re-estimated using these two sub-selections. Appendix O shows the corresponding results.

The estimated coefficients of bearer biological assets sub-selection are statistically similar to those of initial multivariate analysis. In the case of consumable biological assets, the interaction variable is not supported; it seems that investors do not value recognised biological assets in firms that exhibit a higher disclosure level. Usually there is an available market price for consumable biological assets and frequently they are sold in the short term. Therefore, the fair value of consumable biological assets is captured by the market faster when compared to bearer biological assets. Moreover, bearer biological assets are held for an extended period and typically it is more difficult to access the corresponding fair value. Consequently, in this case, mandatory disclosure or any further information is useful, and for that reason, investors value bearer biological assets for firms that reveal a higher disclosure level on biological assets.

In order to reinforce the previous analysis, the Chow test was used to determine whether the coefficients can differ across subgroups (Chow, 1960).[10] There is a structural change in this model, and it is necessary to split data into two sub-selections, meaning that independent variables have a different impact on both bearer biological assets and consumable biological assets subgroups of the whole selection.

Based on this result, it is possible to infer that investors highly distinguish recognised biological assets under fair value between bearer biological assets and consumable biological assets. This evidence supports, to some extent, the recent amendments to IAS 41, which prescribe a different accounting treatment for bearer plants when compared to other biological assets.

Finally, and with the purpose of providing some robustness tests, two additional analyses were conducted. Firstly, Appendix P reveals that the inferences of these equations are not sensitive to using prices as of three or six months after the fiscal year-end, except in the third model. In this case, the interaction variable is not statistically significant when considering price as of six months after fiscal year-end. Secondly, given the fact that biological assets per share represents a wide range of values, equations (10) and (11) were re-estimated, using a sub-selection in which firms below the first quartile in terms of biological assets per share in the selection are excluded. Once more, the results are not sensitive to this change, as presented in Appendix Q.

*Conclusions*

The empirical evidence supports the idea that biological assets measured under the fair value model are value relevant in general. Additionally, a recognised amount of biological assets under the fair value model is more value relevant for firms that reveal a higher disclosure level. Following IAS 41 classification of biological assets, the selection of firms was divided into bearer biological assets and consumable biological assets. Results are similar only for bearer biological assets. Investors value recognised consumable biological assets, but independently from corresponding disclosure level. Usually, for consumable biological assets, there is a quoted price in the market and usually they are sold in the short term. Consequently and when compared to bearer biological assets, fair value of consumable biological assets is apprehended more quickly by the market. In the case of bearer biological assets, they are held for an extended period and frequently, it is more difficult to access the corresponding fair value. Accordingly, in this case, mandatory disclosure or any additional information is helpful, and therefore the investors value bearer biological assets for firms that exhibit a higher disclosure level of these assets.

# Notes

1 DataStream is a global financial and macroeconomics time series database that allows users to identify and examine trends, generate and test ideas and develop viewpoints on the market.
2 The analysis of the annual reports was performed by one researcher. In order to assure robustness of the index calculation and to minimise possible coding bias, the researcher coded the information twice and any discrepancies were solved.
3 Regarding the research topic – disclosure – the disclosure score is 40. Regarding the research topic – value relevance – the disclosure score is 27, further explained in the section on fair value relevance.
4 Complete information about the total sample of 270 firms is presented in Appendix D.
5 Complete information about the total sample of 324 firms is presented in Appendix H.
6 There are seven missing firm-year observations, six observations regarding the market value per share variable (the corresponding data are not available in DataStream) and one observation was removed from the earnings per share variable because it was identified as an outlier.

7  Because the fiscal year-end diverges between selected firms (31 March, 30 April, 31 May, 30 June, 31 August, 30 September, 30 November and 31 December, according to WS05350 – date of fiscal year-end), the market value per share (MV) variable was settled according to these dates (WS05040 – June, WS05045 – July, WS05050 – August, WS05055 – September, WS05065 – November, WS05070 – December, WS05020 – February and WS05025 – March). For example, WS05040 – market price June close corresponds to market value per share three months after fiscal year-end on 31 March.

8  Complete information about the total sample of 132 firms is presented in Appendix D.

9  In this test the null hypothesis is that the coefficients estimated by the random effects estimator are the same as those estimated by the fixed effects estimator.

10  Due to the fact that the F-statistic is 5.798, which is superior to its critical value of 2.369 at 1% level of significance, the study rejects the null hypothesis of structural stability.

# 6 Main findings and future avenues of research

This book provides important contributions to literature on biological assets under IAS 41. Compared to previous studies, this research analysed a wider selection of firms, ensuring that a larger number of countries and drivers related to disclosure and measurement are taken into consideration.

In general, this study contributes to the extension of the current knowledge of biological assets disclosure level, disclosure and measurement drivers and constraints. In addition, particular attention is given to the market valuation implications of this standard.

Regarding disclosure practices, empirical results suggest that the mandatory and voluntary disclosure level is influenced by biological assets intensity, ownership concentration, firm size, sector and legal status. Two main findings corroborate earlier studies: the need to improve the disclosure level and the dichotomy of common law versus code law countries. In general, IAS 41 requires biological assets to be measured at fair value less costs to sell. Ideally, firms that measure biological assets at historical cost should correspond to firms with no conditions to report biological assets at fair value. This book supports previous studies that claim that other reasons exist related to firm and country environment that can explain the adoption of historical cost, even when the unreliability clause of fair value does not apply. Considering measurement practices, evidence shows that fair value adoption is influenced by biological assets intensity, firm size, listing status, regulation expertise, potential growth, sector and legal status.

In terms of value relevance, this research suggests that biological assets at fair value are value relevant, in particular for firms that show a higher disclosure level. Following the division between bearer and consumable biological assets, results are only similar for bearer biological assets. There is usually an available market price for consumable biological assets and these biological assets are usually sold in the short term. Therefore, investors value recognised, consumable biological assets, but independently from the corresponding disclosure level. Bearer biological assets are held for an extended period and typically it is more difficult to access the corresponding fair value. Consequently, any further information is useful, so investors value bearer biological assets for firms that show a higher disclosure level on biological assets.

Overall, the key message is standardisation, emphasising the need to improve the disclosure level of listed firms and to eliminate the uncertainty in the understanding of IAS 41. The evidence supports low disclosure levels, low comparability and also supports the discretion of firms where measurement of biological assets is concerned.

In particular, this study has contributed in supporting policy makers and international standard setters involved in future reviews of IAS 41. The empirical evidence provided in this book supports the recent amendments of IAS 41, especially the different models applied to consumable and bearer biological assets. As such, it is the author's belief that further academic research or further projects of IASB could be extended to other bearer biological assets, rather than plants, in order to apply or not apply the same amendments.

Several possible extensions of the empirical studies included in the book are envisaged and other classifications regarding firms or countries could be explored. Additionally, other links could be developed, such as the relationship between the measurement and disclosure practices in this domain. Furthermore, the impact of environmental regulations at the country level could be analysed in terms of how it influences the firms' incentives to disclose information and to adopt fair value with respect to IAS 41. With regard to the value relevance of biological assets, further research could replicate this analysis to ascertain whether the results hold consistently across additional countries that adopted IFRS after 2010 and 2011. It could also be useful to investigate the extent to which market assessments of recognised versus disclosed biological asset amounts depend on the method of valuation (historical cost versus fair value).

# References

Abraham, S. and P. J. Shrives (2014), "Improving the relevance of risk factor disclosure in corporate annual reports", *The British Accounting Review*, Vol. 46, No. 1, pp. 91–107.

Ahmed, A. S., E. Kilic and G. J. Lobo (2006), "Does recognition versus disclosure matter? Evidence from value-relevance of banks' recognized and disclosed derivative financial instruments", *Accounting Review*, Vol. 81, No. 3, pp. 567–588.

Akhtaruddin, M. (2005), "Corporate mandatory disclosure practices in Bangladesh", *The International Journal of Accounting*, Vol. 40, No. 4, pp. 399–422.

Al Jifri, K. and D. Citron (2009), "The value-relevance of financial statement recognition versus note disclosure: evidence from goodwill accounting", *European Accounting Review*, Vol. 18, No. 1, pp. 123–140.

Amiraslani, H., G. E. Iatridis and P. F. Pope (2013), "Accounting for asset impairment: a test for IFRS compliance across Europe", a research report of the Centre for Financial Analysis and Reporting Research, Cass Business School. Last accessed on 16 June 2017, www.cass.city.ac.uk/__data/assets/pdf_file/0019/160075/CeFARR-Impairment-Research-Report.pdf

Argilés, J. M., J. Garcia-Blandón and T. Monllau (2009), "Fair value versus historic cost valuation for biological assets: implications for the quality of financial information". Last accessed on 16 June 2017, www.ub.edu/ubeconomics/wp-content/uploads/2013/06/215.pdf

Argilés, J. M., J. Garcia-Blandon and T. Monllau (2011), "Fair value versus historical cost-based valuation for biological assets: predictability of financial information", *Revista de Contabilidad*, Vol. 14, No. 2, pp. 87–113.

Argilés, J. M. and E. J. Slof (2001), "New opportunities for farm accounting", *European Accounting Review*, Vol. 10, No. 2, pp. 361–383.

Argilés Bosh, J. M., A. Sabata Aliberch and J. Garcia-Blandon (2012), "A comparative study of difficulties in accounting preparation and judgment in agriculture using fair value and historical cost for biological assets valuation", *Revista de Contabilidad*, Vol. 15, No. 1, pp. 109–142.

Baboukardos, D. and G. Rimmel (2014), "Goodwill under IFRS: relevance and disclosures in an unfavorable environment", *Accounting Forum*, Vol. 38, No. 1, pp. 1–17.

Badenhorst, W. M., L. M. Brümmer and J. H. V. De Wet (2015), "The value-relevance of disclosed summarised financial information of listed associates", *Journal of International Accounting, Auditing and Taxation*, Vol. 24, pp. 1–12.

Ball, R. (2006), "International Financial Reporting Standards (IFRS): pros and cons for investors", *Accounting & Business Research (Wolters Kluwer UK)*, Vol. 36, pp. 5–27.

Barlev, B. and J. R. Haddad (2003), "Fair value accounting and the management of the firm", *Critical Perspectives on Accounting*, Vol. 14, No. 4, pp. 383–415.

Barth, M. E., W. H. Beaver and W. R. Landsman (2001), "The relevance of the value relevance literature for financial accounting standard setting: another view", *Journal of Accounting and Economics*, Vol. 31, No. 1–3, pp. 77–104.

Barth, M. E. and G. Clinch (1998), "Revalued financial, tangible, and intangible assets: associations with share prices and non-market-based value estimates", *Journal of Accounting Research*, Vol. 36, pp. 199–233.

(2009), "Scale effects in capital markets-based accounting research", *Journal of Business Finance & Accounting*, Vol. 36, No. 3–4, pp. 253–288.

Barth, M. E., G. Clinch and T. Shibano (2003), "Market effects of recognition and disclosure", *Journal of Accounting Research*, Vol. 41, No. 4, pp. 581–609.

Barth, M. and D. Israeli (2013), "Disentangling mandatory IFRS reporting and changes in enforcement", *Journal of Accounting and Economics*, Vol. 56 (No. 2–3, Supplement 1), pp. 178–188.

Bellora, L. and T. W. Guenther (2013), "Drivers of innovation capital disclosure in intellectual capital statements: evidence from Europe", *The British Accounting Review*, Vol. 45, No. 4, pp. 255–270.

Black, F. and M. Scholes (1973), "The pricing of options and corporate liabilities", *The Journal of Political Economy*, Vol. 81, No. 3, pp. 637–654.

Brown, P., J. Preiato and A. Tarca (2014), "Enforcement of accounting standards: an audit and enforcement proxy", *Journal of Business Finance & Accounting*, Vol. 41, No. 1 & 2, pp. 1–52.

Cairns, D. (2006), "The use of fair value in IFRS", *Accounting in Europe*, Vol. 3, No. 1, pp. 5–22.

Cairns, D., D. Massoudi, R. Taplin and A. Tarca (2011), "IFRS fair value measurement and accounting policy choice in the United Kingdom and Australia", *The British Accounting Review*, Vol. 43, No. 1, pp. 1–21.

Callao Gastón, S., C. Ferrer García, J. I. Jarne Jarne and J. A. Laínez Gadea (2010), "IFRS adoption in Spain and the United Kingdom: effects on accounting numbers and relevance", *Advances in Accounting*, Vol. 26, No. 2, pp. 304–313.

Carmona, S. and M. Trombetta (2008), "On the global acceptance of IAS/IFRS accounting standards: The logic and implications of the principles-based system", *Journal of Accounting and Public Policy*, Vol. 27, No. 6, pp. 455–461.

Cascino, S. and J. Gassen (2011), "Comparability effects of mandatory IFRS adoption". Last accessed on 16 June 2017, http://ideas.repec.org/p/hum/wpaper/sfb649dp2012-009.html

Chalmers, K. and J. M. Godfrey (2004), "Reputation costs: the impetus for voluntary derivative financial instrument reporting", *Accounting, Organizations and Society*, Vol. 29, No. 2, pp. 95–125.

Chavent, M., Y. Ding, L. Fu, H. Stolowy and H. Wang (2006), "Disclosure and determinants studies: an extension using the Divisive Clustering Method (DIV)", *European Accounting Review*, Vol. 15, No. 2, pp. 181–218.

Choudhary, P. (2011), "Evidence on differences between recognition and disclosure: a comparison of inputs to estimate fair values of employee stock options", *Journal of Accounting and Economics*, Vol. 51, No. 1–2, pp. 77–94.

Chow, G. (1960), "Tests of equality between sets of coefficients in two linear regressions", *Econometrica*, Vol. 28, No. 3, pp. 591–605.

Christensen, H. B. and V. V. Nikolaev (2013), "Does fair value accounting for non-financial assets pass the market test?", *Review of Accounting Studies*, Vol. 18, No. 3, pp. 734–775.

CIA (2015), "The World Factbook". Last accessed on 16 June 2017, www.cia.gov/library/publications/the-world-factbook/fields/2100.html

Commission Regulation (EU) no. 1255/2012 of 11 December 2012. Available at http://eur-lex.europa.eu

Conceptual Framework for Financial Reporting of IASB. Available at www.ifrs.org

Cooke, T. E. (1989), "Voluntary corporate disclosure by Swedish companies", *Journal of International Financial Management and Accounting*, Vol. 1, No. 2, pp. 171–195.

——— (1992), "The impact of size, stock market listing and industry type on disclosure in the annual reports of Japanese listed corporations", *Accounting and Business Research (Wolters Kluwer UK)*, Vol. 22, No. 87, pp. 229–237.

Daniel, S., B. Jung, H. Pourjalali and E. Wen (2010), "Firm characteristics influencing responses towards adoption of the fair value accounting option: a survey of chief financial officers of U.S. firms". Last accessed on 16 June 2017, http://ssrn.com/abstract=1579326

Daske, H., L. Hail, C. Leuz and R. Verdi (2013), "Adopting a label: heterogeneity in the economic consequences around IAS/IFRS adoptions", *Journal of Accounting Research*, Vol. 51, No. 3, pp. 495–547.

Davis-Friday, P. Y., L. B. Folami, L. Chao-Shin and H. F. Mittelstaedt (1999), "The value relevance of financial statement recognition vs. disclosure: evidence from SFAS no. 106", *Accounting Review*, Vol. 74, No. 4, pp. 403–423.

DeAngelo, L. E. (1981), "Auditor size and audit quality", *Journal of Accounting and Economics*, Vol. 3, No. 3, pp. 183–199.

Demaria, S. and D. Dufour (2007), "First time adoption of IFRS, fair value option, conservatism: evidences from French listed companies", in EAA 30th doctoral colloquium in accounting. Last accessed on 16 June 2017, http://halshs.archives-ouvertes.fr/halshs-00266189

Depoers, F. (2000), "A cost-benefit study of voluntary disclosure: some empirical evidence from French listed companies", *European Accounting Review*, Vol. 9, No. 2, pp. 245–263.

Ding, Y., O.-K. Hope, T. Jeanjean and H. Stolowy (2007), "Differences between domestic accounting standards and IAS: measurement, determinants and implications", *Journal of Accounting and Public Policy*, Vol. 26, pp. 1–38.

Djankov, S., E. Glaeser, R. La Porta, F. Lopez-de-Silanes and A. Shleifer (2003), "The new comparative economics", *Journal of Comparative Economics*, Vol. 31, No. 4, pp. 595–619.

Doupnik, T. S. and S. B. Salter (1995), "External environment, culture and accounting practice: a preliminary test of a general model of international accounting development", *International Journal of Accounting*, Vol. 30, No. 3, pp. 189–207.

Elad, C. (2004), "Fair value accounting in the agricultural sector: some implications for international accounting harmonization", *European Accounting Review*, Vol. 13, No. 4, pp. 621–641.

Elad, C. and K. Herbohn (2011), "Implementing fair value accounting in the agricultural sector". Last accessed on 16 June 2017, www.icas.com/__data/assets/pdf_file/0019/10549/10-Implementing-Fair-Value-Accounting-In-The-Agricultural-Sector-ICAS.pdf

European Commission (2014), "Endorsement of amendments to IAS 16 and IAS 41 – *Agriculture: Bearer Plants*". Last accessed on 16 June 2017, https://ec.europa.eu/info/sites/info/files/cover-letter-bearer-plants_en.pdf

Fama, E. and M. Jensen (1983), "Separation of ownership and control", *Journal of Law and Economics*, Vol. 26, pp. 1–31.

Fargher, N. and J. Z. Zhang (2014), "Changes in the measurement of fair value: implications for accounting earnings", *Accounting Forum*, Vol. 38, No. 3, pp. 184–199.

Fields, T. D., T. Z. Lys and L. Vincent (2001), "Empirical research on accounting choice", *Journal of Accounting and Economics*, Vol. 31, No. 1–3, pp. 255–307.

Fisher, R., T. Mortensen and D. Webber (2010), "Fair value accounting in the agricultural sector: an analysis of financial statement preparers' perceptions before and after the introduction of IAS 41 agriculture". 2010 *Accounting & Finance Association of Australia and New Zealand Conference Proceedings*, Christchurch, New Zealand, 4–6 July. Last accessed on 16 June 2017, www.afaanz.org/openconf/2010/modules/request.php?module=oc_proceedings&action=proceedings.php&a=Accept+as+Paper

Fried, A. N. (2012), "Disclosure versus recognition: evidence from lobbying behavior in response to SFAS no. 158", *Research in Accounting Regulation*, Vol. 24, No. 1, pp. 25–32.

Gabriel, N. C. and P. Stefea (2013), "International Accounting Standard 41 (IAS 41) – implication for reporting crop assets", *Lucrări Ştiinţifice Management Agricol*, Vol. 15, No. 3, pp. 100–105.

George, M. S. C. (2007), "Why fair value needs felling", *Accountancy*, Vol. 139, No. 1365, pp. 80–81.

George, E., X. Li and L. Shivakumar (2016), "A review of the IFRS adoption literature", *Review of Accounting Studies*, Vol. 21, pp. 898–1004.

Glaum, M., P. Schmidt, D. L. Street and S. Vogel (2013), "Compliance with IFRS 3- and IAS 36-required disclosures across 17 European countries: company- and country-level determinants", *Accounting and Business Research*, Vol. 43, No. 3, pp. 163–204.

Greene, W. H. (2012), *Econometric Analysis* (7th edition). Prentice Hall.

Gujarati, D. N. (1995), *Basic Econometrics* (3rd edition). McGraw-Hill International editions.

Guo, L. and Y. Yang (2013), "Study on measurement attributes of biological assets in Chinese agribusiness", in *Informatics and Management Science IV*, pp. 323–328.

Hail, L., C. Leuz and P. Wysocki (2010), "Global accounting convergence and the potential adoption of IFRS by the U.S. (part II): political factors and future scenarios for U.S. accounting standards", *Accounting Horizons*, Vol. 24, No. 4, pp. 567–588.

Hamberg, M. and L.-A. Beisland (2014), "Changes in the value relevance of goodwill accounting following the adoption of IFRS 3", *Journal of Accounting, Auditing and Taxation*, Vol. 23, No. 2, pp. 59–73.

Healy, P. M. and K. G. Palepu (2001), "Information asymmetry, corporate disclosure, and the capital markets: a review of the empirical disclosure literature", *Journal of Accounting and Economics*, Vol. 31, pp. 405–440.

Heitzman, S., C. Wasley and J. Zimmerman (2010), "The joint effects of materiality thresholds and voluntary disclosure incentives on firms' disclosure decisions", *Journal of Accounting and Economics*, Vol. 49, No. 1–2, pp. 109–132.

Hellmann, A., H. Perera and C. Patel (2013), "Continental European accounting model and accounting modernization in Germany", *Advances in Accounting: Incorporating Advances in International Accounting*, Vol. 29, No. 1, pp. 124–133.

Herbohn, K. and J. Herbohn. (2006), "International Accounting Standard (IAS) 41: what are the implications for reporting forest assets? Small-scale forest economics", *Management and Policy*, Vol. 5, No. 2, pp. 175–189.

Herbohn, K. F., R. Peterson and J. L. Herbohn (1998), "Accounting for forestry assets: current practice and future directions", *Australian Accounting Review*, Vol. 8, No. 15, pp. 54–66.

Hitz, J.-M. (2007), "The decision usefulness of fair value accounting – a theoretical perspective", *European Accounting Review*, Vol. 16, No. 2, pp. 323–362.

Hlaing, K. P. and H. Pourjalali (2012), "Economic reasons for reporting property, plant, and equipment at fair market value by foreign cross-listed firms in the United States", *Journal of Accounting, Auditing and Finance*, Vol. 27, No. 4, pp. 557–576.

Hodgdon, C., R. H. Tondkar, A. Adhikari and D. W. Harless (2009), "Compliance with International Financial Reporting Standards and auditor choice: new evidence on the importance of the statutory audit", *The International Journal of Accounting*, Vol. 44, No. 1, pp. 33–55.

Holthausen, R. W. and R. L. Watts (2001), "The relevance of the value-relevance literature for financial accounting standard setting", *Journal of Accounting and Economics*, Vol. 31, No. 1–3, pp. 3–75.

Hooks, J. and C. J. Van Staden (2011), "Evaluating environmental disclosures: the relationship between quality and extent measures", *The British Accounting Review*, Vol. 43, No. 3, pp. 200–213.

Hope, O.-K. (2003), "Disclosure practices, enforcement of accounting standards, and analysts' forecast accuracy: an international study", *Journal of Accounting Research*, Vol. 41, No. 2, pp. 235–272.

Hosmer, D. W. Jr., S. Lemeshow and R. X. Sturdivant (2013), *Applied Logistic Regression* (3rd edition). John Wiley & Sons, Inc.

Huffman, A. A. (2013), "Value relevant asset measurement and asset use: evidence from IAS 41". Last accessed on 16 June 2017, http://eifrs.ifrs.org/eifrs/comment_letters/27/27_3206_AdriennaHuffmanUniversityofUtah_2_HuffmanAdriennaJobMarketPaper.pdf

IAS 41 Agriculture. Available at www.ifrs.org

IFRS 13 Fair value measurement. Available at www.ifrs.org

IFRS Foundation (2013), "Breaking the boilerplate", Speech by Hans Hoogervorst. Last accessed on 16 June 2017, https://dart.deloitte.com/resource/1/eff58b14-3f32-11e6-95db-6b4f3ddff7f9

Inchausti, B. G. (1997), "The influence of company characteristics and accounting regulation on information disclosed by Spanish firms", *European Accounting Review*, Vol. 6, No. 1, pp. 45–68.

Jackson, E. and M. Roe (2009), "Public and private enforcement of securities laws: Resource-based evidence", *Journal of Financial Economics*, Vol. 93, No. 2, pp. 207–238.

Jensen, M. C. and W. H. Meckling (1976), "Theory of the firm: managerial behaviour, agency costs and ownership structure", *Journal of Financial Economics*, Vol. 3, No. 4, pp. 305–360.

Kaufmann, D., A. Kraay and M. Mastruzzi (2011), "The worldwide governance indicators: methodology and analytical issues", *Hague Journal on the Rule of Law*, Vol. 3, pp. 220–246.

Kun, Y. (2013), "Does recognition versus disclosure affect value relevance? Evidence from pension accounting", *Accounting Review*, Vol. 88, No. 3, pp. 1095–1127.

La Porta, R., F. Lopez-de-Silanes, A. Shleifer and R. W. Vishny (1998), "Law and finance", *Journal of Political Economy*, Vol. 106, No. 6, pp. 1113–1155.

Lan, Y., L. Wang and X. Zhang (2013), "Determinants and features of voluntary disclosure in the Chinese stock market", *China Journal of Accounting Research*, Vol. 6, No. 4, pp. 265–285.

Lang, M. and R. Lundholm (1993), "Cross-sectional determinants of analyst ratings of corporate disclosure", *Journal of Accounting Research*, Vol. 31, No. 2, pp. 246–271.

Laux, C. and C. Leuz (2010), "Did fair-value accounting contribute to the financial crisis?", *Journal of Economic Perspectives*, Vol. 24, No. 1, pp. 93–118.

Lefter, V. and A. Roman (2007), "IAS 41: fair value accounting", *Theoretical and Applied Economics*, Vol. 5, No. 50, pp. 15–22.

Leuz, C. (2010), "Different approaches to corporate reporting regulation: how jurisdictions differ and why", *Accounting and Business Research*, Vol. 40, No. 3, pp. 229–256.

Leuz, C. and P. D. Wysocki (2008), "Economic consequences of financial reporting and disclosure regulation: a review and suggestions for future research". Last accessed on 16 June 2017, http://ssrn.com/abstract=1105398

Lewis, P. and S. Salter (2006), "Europe and America – together or apart: an empirical test of differences in actual reported results", *Advances in International Accounting*, Vol. 19, pp. 221–242.

Littleton, A. C. (1935), "Value or cost", The Accounting Review, Vol. 10, No. 3, pp. 269–273.

Lindahl, F. and H. Schadéwitz (2013), "Are legal families related to financial reporting quality?", *Abacus*, Vol. 49, No. 2, pp. 242–267.

Lopes, P. T. and L. L. Rodrigues (2007), "Accounting for financial instruments: an analysis of the determinants of disclosure in the Portuguese stock exchange", *The International Journal of Accounting*, Vol. 42, pp. 25–56.

Lourenço, I. and J. D. Curto (2008), "The value relevance of investment property fair values". Last accessed on 16 June 2017, http://ssrn.com/abstract=1301683

Luft, J. and M. D. Shields (2014), "Subjectivity in developing and validating causal explanations in positivist accounting research", *Accounting, Organizations and Society*, Vol. 39, pp. 550–558.

Machado, M. J. C., E. A. Martins and L. N. Carvalho (2015), "Reliability in fair value of assets without an active market", *Advances in Scientific and Applied Accounting*, Vol. 7, No. 3, pp. 319–338.

Mala, R. and P. Chand (2012), "Effect of the global financial crisis on accounting convergence", *Accounting & Finance*, Vol. 52, No. 1, pp. 21–46.

Marston, C. L. and P. J. Shrives (1991), "The use of disclosure indices in accounting research: a review article", *British Accounting Review*, Vol. 23, No. 3, pp. 195–210.

Martins, A. I. S., R. M. P. Almeida and T. A. Jesus (2012), "O impacte da IAS 41 e o seu valor relevante nas empresas agrícolas cotadas", *Revista Portuguesa de Contabilidade*, Vol. 2, No. 8, pp. 577–616.

Missonier-Piera, F. (2007), "Motives for fixed-asset revaluation: an empirical analysis with Swiss data", *The International Journal of Accounting*, Vol. 42, pp. 186–205.

Morris, R. (1987), "Signalling, agency theory and accounting policy choice", *Accounting & Business Research*, Vol. 18, No. 69, pp. 47–56.

Muller, K. A., E. J. Riedl and T. Sellhorn (2008), "Causes and consequences of choosing historical cost versus fair value". Last accessed on 16 June 2017, http://care-mendoza.nd.edu/assets/152281/riedlmrs03062008.pdf

Myers, S. C. (1977), "Determinants of corporate borrowing", *Journal of Financial Economics*, Vol. 5, pp. 147–175.

Nobes, C. (2008), "Accounting classification in the IFRS era", *Australian Accounting Review*, No. 46, Vol. 18, Issue 3, pp. 191–198.

Nobes, C. and C. Stadler (2013), "How arbitrary are international accounting classifications? Lessons from centuries of classifying in many disciplines, and experiments with IFRS data", *Accounting, Organizations and Society*, Vol. 38, No. 8, pp. 573–595.

Ohlson, J. A. (1995), "Earnings, book values and dividends in equity valuation", *Contemporary Accounting Research*, Vol. 11, No. 2, pp. 661–687.

Oliveira, J. D. S., G. M. D. C. Azevedo, C. D. S. A. Santos and S. C. S. Vasconcelos (2015), "Fair value: model proposal for the dairy sector", *Agricultural Finance Review*, Vol. 75, No. 2, pp. 230–252.

Oliveira, L., L. L. Rodrigues and R. Craig (2006), "Firm-specific determinants of intangibles reporting: evidence from the Portuguese stock market", *Journal of Human Resource Costing & Accounting*, Vol. 10, No. 1, pp. 11–33.

——— (2010), "Intangible assets and value relevance: evidence from the Portuguese stock exchange", *The British Accounting Review*, Vol. 42, No. 4, pp. 241–252.

Owusu-Ansah, S. (1998), "The impact of corporate attributes on the extent of mandatory disclosure and reporting by listed companies in Zimbabwe", *The International Journal of Accounting*, Vol. 33, No. 5, pp. 605–631.

Peng, C., K. Lee and G. Ingersoll (2002), "An introduction to logistic regression analysis and reporting", *The Journal of Educational Research*, Vol. 96, No. 1, pp. 3–14.

Preiato, J., P. Brown and A. Tarca (2015), A comparison of between-country measures of legal setting and enforcement of accounting standards. *Journal of Business Finance & Accounting*, Vol. 42, No. 1 & 2, pp. 1–50.

PwC (2009), "Forest industry: application review of IAS 41, agriculture: the fair value of standing timber". Last accessed on 16 June 2017, www.pwc.com/gx/en/industries/forest-paper-packaging/publications/ias-41.html

——— (2011), "IAS 41, agriculture: the fair value of standing timber: 2011 update". Last accessed on 16 June 2017, www.pwc.com/gx/en/industries/forest-paper-packaging/publications/ias41-fair-value-timber-form.html

Quagli, A. and F. Avallone (2010), "Fair value or cost model? Drivers of choice for IAS 40 in the real estate industry", *European Accounting Review*, Vol. 19, No. 3, pp. 461–493.

Rahman, A., H. Perera and S. Ganesh (2002), "Accounting practice harmony accounting regulation and firm characteristics", *Abacus*, Vol. 38, No. 1, pp. 46–77.

Regulation (EC) no. 1606/2002 of 19 July 2002. Last accessed on 16 June 2017, http://eur-lex.europa.eu

Samudhram, A., E. Stewart, J. Wickramanayake and J. Sinnakkannu (2014), "Value relevance of human capital based disclosures: moderating effects of labor productivity, investor sentiment, analyst coverage and audit quality", *Advances in Accounting*, Vol. 30, No. 2, pp. 338–353.

Santos, E. S., V. Ponte and P. V. R. Mapurunga (2013), "Mandatory IFRS adoption in Brazil (2010): index of compliance with disclosure requirements and explanatory factors of firms reporting". Last accessed on 16 June 2017, http://dx.doi.org/10.2139/ssrn.2310625

Scherch, C. P., D. R. Nogueira, P. A. Olak and C. V. O. A. Cruz (2013), "Nível de conformidade do cpc 29 nas empresas brasileiras: uma análise com as empresas de capital aberto", *Revista de Administração, Contabilidade e Economia*, Vol. 12, No. 2, pp. 459–490.

Shalev, R. (2009), "The information content of business combination disclosure level", *Accounting Review*, Vol. 84, No. 1, pp. 239–270.

Silva, R. M., L. Figueira, L. Pereira and M. S. Ribeiro (2012), "Process of convergence to the international financial reporting standards: an analysis of the disclosure requirements of CPC 29/IAS 41". Last accessed on 16 June 2017, http://dx.doi.org/10.2139/ssrn.2012705

Steenkamp, N. and D. Northcott (2007), "Content analysis in accounting research: the practical challenges", *Australian Accounting Review*, Vol. 17, pp. 12–25.

Stefano, C. and J. Gassen (2015), "What drives the comparability effect of mandatory IFRS adoption?", *Review of Accounting Studies*, Vol. 20, pp. 242–282.

Stone, M. and J. Rasp (1991), "Tradeoffs in the choice between logit and ols for accounting choice studies", *The Accounting Review*, Vol. 66, No. 1, pp. 170–187.

Taplin, R., W. Yuan and A. Brown (2014), "The use of fair value and historical cost: accounting for investment properties in China", *Australasian Accounting, Business and Finance Journal*, Vol. 8, No. 1, pp. 101–113.

Theiss, V., M. J. S. Utzig, P. S. Varela and I. M. Beuren (2012), "Práticas de divulgação dos ativos biológicos pelas companhias listadas na bm&fbovespa", *Registro Contábil*, Vol. 5, No. 3, pp. 41–58.

Tsalavoutas, I. (2011), "Transition to IFRS and compliance with mandatory disclosure requirements: what is the signal?", *Advances in Accounting*, Vol. 27, No. 2, pp. 390–405.

Tsalavoutas, I., P. André and D. Dionysiou (2014), "Worldwide application of IFRS 3, IAS 38 and IAS 36, related disclosures, and determinants of non-compliance", ACCA Research report 134. Last accessed on 16 June 2017, www.accaglobal.com/content/dam/acca/global/PDF-technical/financial-reporting/rr-134-001.pdf

Tsalavoutas, I. and D. Dionysiou (2014), "Value relevance of IFRS mandatory disclosure requirements", *Journal of Applied Accounting Research*, Vol. 15, pp. 22–42.

Tsoligkas, F. and I. Tsalavoutas (2011), "Value relevance of R&D in the UK after IFRS mandatory implementation", *Applied Financial Economics*, Vol. 21, pp. 957–967.

Van Staden, C. J. and J. Hooks (2007), "A comprehensive comparison of corporate environmental reporting and responsiveness", *The British Accounting Review*, Vol. 39, pp. 197–210.

Watts, R. L. (1992), "Accounting choice theory and market-based research in accounting", *British Accounting Review*, Vol. 24, pp. 235–267.

Watts, R. L. and J. L. Zimmerman (1983), "Agency problems, auditing, and the theory of the firm: some evidence", *Journal of Law and Economics*, Vol. 26, No. 3, pp. 613–633.

(1990), "Positive accounting theory: a ten year perspective", *Accounting Review*, Vol. 65, No. 1, pp. 131–156.

White, H. (1980), "A heteroskedasticity-consistent covariance matrix estimator and a direct test for heteroskedasticity", *Econometrica*, Vol. 48, No. 4, pp. 817–838.

Wysocki, P. (2011), "New institutional accounting and IFRS", *Accounting and Business Research*, Vol. 4, No. 3, pp. 309–328.

Zmijewski, M. E. and R. L. Hagerman (1981), "An income strategy approach to the positive theory of accounting standard setting/choice", *Journal of Accounting and Economics*, Vol. 3, No. 2, pp. 129–149.

# Appendices

| § | Score | Disclosure index | Disclosure level by item | |
|---|---|---|---|---|
| | | | Disclosure 270 firms 2011 | Value relevance 132 firms 2011–2013 |
| *Mandatory items – the entity discloses:* | | | | |
| **40** | | Aggregate gain or loss arising during the current period: | | |
| **40** | 1 | On initial recognition of biological assets | 14 | 27 |
| **40** | 1 | On initial recognition of agricultural produce | 5 | 9 |
| **40** | 1 | From the change in fair value less costs to sell of biological assets | 201 | 348 |
| **41** | 1 | Description of each group of biological assets | 230 | 345 |
| **42** | 1 | Description in [IAS 41.41] is narrative | 174 | 281 |
| **42** | 1 | Description in [IAS 41.41] is quantified | 204 | 287 |
| **46** | 1 | Description of an entity's activities involving each group of biological assets | 123 | 207 |
| **46** | | Description of non-financial measures or estimates of the physical quantities of: | | |
| **46** | 1 | Each group of the entity's biological assets at the end of the period | 156 | 225 |

(*continued*)

| § | Score | Disclosure index | Disclosure level by item | |
|---|---|---|---|---|
| | | | Disclosure 270 firms 2011 | Value relevance 132 firms 2011–2013 |
| **46** | **1** | Output of agricultural produce during the period | 60 | 103 |
| **47** | **1/(NA)**[a] | Methods and significant assumptions applied in determining the fair value of each group of agricultural produce at the point of harvest and of biological assets | 109 | 130 |
| **48** | **1/(NA)**[a] | Fair value less costs to sell of agricultural produce harvested during the period, determined at the point of harvest | 112 | 131 |
| **49** | **1** | Information about biological assets whose title is restricted or pledged as security | 38 | 55 |
| **49** | **1** | Amount of commitments for developing or acquiring biological assets | 24 | 42 |
| **49** | **1** | Financial risk management strategies related to agricultural activity | 88 | 109 |
| **50** | **1** | Reconciliation of changes in the carrying amount of biological assets, between the beginning and the end of the period | 248 | 368 |
| **50** | **1** | This reconciliation includes desegregation | 242 | 368 |

**Additional disclosures when the fair value cannot be measured reliably**

| | | | | |
|---|---|---|---|---|
| **54** | | The entity measures biological assets at their cost less any accumulated depreciation and any accumulated impairment losses – *the entity discloses:* | | |
| **54** | **1** [a] | Description of the biological assets | 38 | - |
| **54** | **1** [a] | Explanation of why fair value cannot be measured reliably | 49 | - |

| § | Score | Disclosure index | Disclosure level by item | |
|---|---|---|---|---|
| | | | Disclosure 270 firms 2011 | Value relevance 132 firms 2011–2013 |
| 54 | 1 [a] | Range of estimates within which fair value is highly likely to lie | 2 | - |
| 54 | 1 [a] | Depreciation method used | 26 | - |
| 54 | 1 [a] | Useful lives or the depreciation rates used | 33 | - |
| 54 | 1 [a] | Gross carrying amount and the accumulated depreciation (aggregated with accumulated impairment losses) at the beginning and end of the period | 31 | - |
| 55 | 1 [a] | Gain or loss recognised on disposal of biological assets | 7 | - |
| 55 | 1 [a] | Impairment losses, in case of disposal | 0 | - |
| 55 | 1 [a] | Reversals of impairment losses, in case of disposal | 0 | - |
| 55 | 1 [a] | Depreciation, in case of disposal | 12 | - |
| 56 | | Fair value of biological assets previously measured at cost less any accumulated depreciation and impairment losses becomes reliably measurable during the current period – *the entity discloses:* | | |
| 56 | 1 [a] | Description of the biological assets | 0 | - |
| 56 | 1 [a] | Explanation of why fair value has become reliably measurable | 0 | - |
| 56 | 1 [a] | Effect of the change | 0 | - |
| 57 | | Government grants – *the entity discloses:* | | |
| 57 | 1 | Government grants | 26 | 36 |
| 57 | 1 | Nature and extent of government grants recognised in the financial statements | 10 | 12 |

(*continued*)

*Appendix A. (cont.)*

| § | Score | Disclosure index | Disclosure level by item | |
|---|---|---|---|---|
| | | | Disclosure 270 firms 2011 | Value relevance 132 firms 2011–2013 |
| **57** | **1** | Unfulfilled conditions and other contingencies attaching to government grants | 1 | 0 |
| **57** | **1** | Significant decreases expected in the level of government grants | 0 | 0 |

*Non-mandatory but recommended items – the entity discloses:*

| | | | | |
|---|---|---|---|---|
| **43** | | Quantified description of each group of biological assets distinguishing between: | | |
| **43** | **1** | Consumable and bearer biological assets | 56 | 75 |
| **43** | **1** | Mature and immature biological assets | 77 | 125 |
| **51** | **1** | Amount of change in fair value less costs to sell included in profit or loss due to physical changes and due to price changes | 78 | 102 |
| **51** | **1** | This information is presented by the group of biological assets | 33 | 42 |

*Non-mandatory and non-recommended items – the entity discloses:*

| | | | | |
|---|---|---|---|---|
| **NA** | **1** | Complexity of various parameters regarding the effect on the valuation (but there is limited information regarding the effect on the valuation) | 124 | 238 |
| **NA** | **1** | Information on the effects of variations in key factors | 53 | 103 |
| **NA** | **1** | Assumptions on future prices and costs, as well as disclosing a sensitivity analysis with multiple parameters | 47 | 90 |
| | **40** [a] | | | |

a Regarding the research topic – value relevance – the disclosure score is 27, once the disclosure items of IAS 41 that focus on the historical cost were omitted; in particular for 2013, the disclosure score is 27 or 25, depending on the adoption of IFRS 13 by the firms of the selection.

*Appendix B.* Proxies, description and expected signals

| Proxies | Description | Expected signals | Research topic |
|---|---|---|---|
| Biological assets intensity | BIO – Biological assets (WS18277, WS18278, or WS18258) divided by total assets (WS02999) multiplied by 100 | Positive | Disclosure Measurement |
| Ownership concentration | HELD – Closely held shares percentage (WS08021) | Negative | Disclosure |
| Firm size | SIZE – Logarithm of the total assets (WS02999) | Positive | Disclosure |
| | | No expected signal | Value relevance Measurement |
| Auditor type | AUDIT – Binary variable based on whether the firm is audited by a Big 4 auditing firm (WS07800) | Positive | Disclosure |
| Internationalisation level | INT – Foreign sales percentage (WS08731) | Positive | Disclosure |
| Listing status | STOCK – Binary variable based on whether the firm is listed in one or more foreign stock exchange (WS05427) | Positive | Disclosure Measurement |
| Profitability | ROE[a] – Pre-tax income (WS01401) divided by common equity (WS03501) multiplied by 100 | No expected signal | Disclosure |
| Sector | SECTOR – Dummy variable based on whether the firm belongs to sector 1, 2 or others regarding sic-code classification (WS07021) | Positive | Disclosure Measurement Value relevance |
| Regulation expertise | IFRS – Logarithm of the number of years that each firm follows IFRS (WS07536) | Positive | Measurement |
| Potential growth | GROWTH – Market capitalisation divided by common equity (WS09704) | No expected signal | Measurement |
| Leverage | LEV – Total liabilities divided (WS03351) by common equity (WS03501) | Positive | Measurement |

*(continued)*

*Appendix B. (cont.)*

| Proxies | Description | Expected signals | Research topic |
|---|---|---|---|
| Legal status | LEGAL[b] – Binary variable based on whether the firm belongs to a common or code law country (La Porta *et al.*, 1998) | Positive | Disclosure |
| | CLUSTER – Dummy variable based on whether the firm belongs to cluster 1, 2 or 3 (Leuz, 2010) | Positive | Disclosure |
| | AUD08 – Logarithm of audit proxy available for 2008 (Brown *et al.*, 2014) | Positive | Disclosure |
| | ENF08 – Logarithm of enforcement proxy available for 2008 (Brown *et al.*, 2014) | Positive | Disclosure |
| | AUD08_ENF08 – Logarithm of audit and enforcement proxy available for 2008 (Brown *et al.*, 2014) | Positive | Disclosure |
| | QUALITY – Governance indicator of the regulatory quality (Kaufmann *et al.*, 2011) | Positive | Measurement |
| Book value per share | BV – Book value divided by outstanding shares at the firm's fiscal year-end (WS05476) | Positive | Value relevance |
| Biological assets per share | BA – Biological assets (WS18277, WS18278 or WS18258) divided by common shares outstanding (WS05301) | No expected signal | Value relevance |
| Earnings per share | E – Net income (WS01751) divided by common shares outstanding (WS05301) | Positive | Value relevance |
| Disclosure index ranking | Dindex – Dummy variable based on whether the disclosure index regarding biological assets of each firm is below 1st quartile, in the middle of both quartiles, or above 3rd quartile of disclosure index distribution (annual report) | Positive | Value relevance |

a ROE – Instead of adopting WS08301 that corresponds directly to return on equity-total %, the purpose of using the ratio between pre-tax income WS01401 and common equity WS03501 was to neglect the tax effect.

b To assure this classification in a few firms whose countries are not considered in both studies, the World Factbook (CIA, 2015) was used as a source of information.

*Appendix C.* Descriptive statistics

| Variables | Mean | Median | Max. | Min. | Std. dev. | Skewness | Observ. | Research topic |
|---|---|---|---|---|---|---|---|---|
| INDEX | 56.55 | 59.00 | 100.00 | 0.00 | 20.90 | -0.43 | 270 | Disclosure |
| | 60.00 | 60.00 | 100.00 | 13.00 | 18.00 | -0.37 | 389 | Value relevance |
| BIO | 11.65 | 4.51 | 95.38 | 0.0(1) | 16.65 | 2.35 | 270 | Disclosure |
| | 8.86 | 2.29 | 92.60 | 0.0(1) | 14.55 | 2.62 | 321 | Measurement |
| HELD | 54.32 | 60.22 | 99.74 | 0.01 | 28.24 | -0.43 | 228 | Disclosure |
| SIZE | 13.02 | 12.87 | 17.84 | 7.27 | 1.86 | 0.07 | 270 | Disclosure |
| | 5.68 | 5.58 | 7.91 | 2.68 | 0.78 | 0.10 | 321 | Measurement |
| | 5.84 | 5.74 | 7.42 | 3.96 | 0.76 | 0.07 | 389 | Value relevance |
| INT | 46.00 | 40.59 | 100.00 | 0.00 | 38.60 | 0.11 | 221 | Disclosure |
| ROE | 8.58 | 9.77 | 52.02 | -57.20 | 16.39 | -0.68 | 256 | Disclosure |
| AUD08 | 1.25 | 1.36 | 1.51 | 0.60 | 0.28 | -1.48 | 247 | Disclosure |
| ENF08 | 1.11 | 1.20 | 1.34 | 0.30 | 0.24 | -0.76 | 247 | Disclosure |
| AUD08_ENF08 | 1.49 | 1.57 | 1.73 | 0.79 | 0.25 | -1.22 | 247 | Disclosure |
| IFRS | 0.73 | 0.78 | 1.04 | 0.30 | 0.21 | -0.84 | 321 | Measurement |
| GROWTH | 1.55 | 1.08 | 16.35 | -3.28 | 1.74 | 3.68 | 321 | Measurement |
| LEV | 1.28 | 0.88 | 16.09 | -4.92 | 1.77 | 4.27 | 321 | Measurement |
| QUALITY | 0.88 | 0.89 | 1.94 | -0.26 | 0.84 | -0.15 | 321 | Measurement |
| MV | 7.62 | 1.41 | 126.53 | 0.01 | 16.19 | 4.24 | 389 | Value Relevance |
| BV | 6.59 | 1.59 | 148.13 | -0.47 | 15.68 | 5.88 | 389 | Value Relevance |
| BV-BA | 4.89 | 1.23 | 92.10 | -1.64 | 11.59 | 5.39 | 389 | Value Relevance |
| BA | 1.70 | 0.16 | 56.68 | 0.0(1) | 5.94 | 6.31 | 389 | Value Relevance |
| E | 0.50 | 0.06 | 13.88 | -13.08 | 1.86 | 2.58 | 389 | Value Relevance |

| | | Frequency | Index | Fair value % | Research topic |
|---|---|---|---|---|---|
| AUDIT | Audited by a non-Big 4 auditing firm | 72 (27%) | 56.00 | - | Disclosure |
| | Audited by a Big 4 auditing firm | 198 (73%) | 57.00 | - | |
| STOCK | Listed on no foreign stock exchange (FSE) | 214 (79%) | 56.00 | - | Disclosure |
| | Listed on one FSE or multi-listing | 56 (21%) | 58.00 | - | |

*(continued)*

*Appendix C. (cont.)*

| | Frequency | Index | Fair value % | Research topic |
|---|---|---|---|---|
| **SECTOR** | | | | |
| Listed on no FSE | 282 (87%) | - | 63.83 | Measurement |
| Listed on one FSE or multi-listing | 41 (13%) | - | 95.12 | |
| No label | 1 (0.3%) | - | 100.00 | |
| Agriculture, forestry, fishing and mining | 86 (32%) | 60.00 | - | Disclosure |
| Manufacturing | 150 (56%) | 57.00 | - | |
| Others | 34 (13%) | 46.00 | - | |
| Agriculture, forestry, fishing and mining | 92 (28%) | - | 78.26 | Measurement |
| Manufacturing | 182 (56%) | - | 60.99 | |
| Others | 50 (15%) | - | 74.00 | |
| Agriculture, forestry, fishing and mining | 46 (35%) | - | - | Value relevance |
| Manufacturing | 63 (48%) | - | - | |
| Others | 23 (17%) | - | - | |
| **LEGAL** | | | | |
| Common law | 107 (40%) | 59.00 | - | Disclosure |
| Code law | 160 (59%) | 55.00 | - | |
| No label | 3 (1%) [a] | 48.00 | - | |
| **CLUSTER** | | | | |
| Cluster 1 | 103 (38%) | 58.00 | - | Disclosure |
| Cluster 2 | 97 (36%) | 58.00 | - | |
| Cluster 3 | 58 (21%) | 53.00 | - | |
| No label | 12 (4%) [b] | 50.00 | - | |
| **FAIR** | | | | |
| Fair value | 220 (68%) | - | - | Measurement |
| Historical cost | 104 (32%) | - | - | |
| **Dindex** | | | | |
| Below quartile 0.25(50) | 98 (25%) | - | - | Value relevance |
| Between quartiles 0.25(50) and 0.75(74) | 202 (51%) | - | - | |
| Above quartile 0.75(74) | 96 (24%) | - | - | |

[a] These firms represent the countries Cyprus, Mauritius and United Arab Emirates. Regarding the World Factbook (CIA, 2015), these countries have a mixed classification: Cyprus and Mauritius correspond to common law/civil law and the United Arab Emirates corresponds to Muslim law/civil law.

[b] These firms represent the countries Cayman Islands, Croatia, Cyprus, Kuwait, Mauritius, Oman, Russian Federation, Ukraine and the United Arab Emirates. These countries are not included in Leuz's (2010) cluster classification. Furthermore, there is no additional information that supports a plausible classification.

*Appendix D.* Ranking of countries by the number of firms and their average disclosure level

| Country | Disclosure | | Value relevance | | | |
|---|---|---|---|---|---|---|
| | Number of firms | Disclosure index | Number of firms | Disclosure index | | |
| | | 2011 | | 2011 | 2012 | 2013 |
| Chile | 30 | 52.00 | 10 | 59.00 | 59.00 | 61.00 |
| Brazil | 28 | 59.00 | 15 | 61.00 | 63.00 | 62.00 |
| Australia | 25 | 63.00 | 16 | 59.00 | 61.00 | 61.00 |
| Hong Kong | 24 | 67.00 | 22 | 57.00 | 57.00 | 60.00 |
| South Africa | 20 | 49.00 | 15 | 57.00 | 58.00 | 59.00 |
| United Kingdom | 17 | 60.00 | 8 | 76.00 | 76.00 | 75.00 |
| China | 11 | 44.00 | - | - | - | - |
| New Zealand | 11 | 64.00 | 6 | 63.00 | 63.00 | 65.00 |
| France | 9 | 52.00 | 4 | 45.00 | 48.00 | 47.00 |
| Norway | 9 | 47.00 | 5 | 58.00 | 58.00 | 62.00 |
| Philippines | 8 | 49.00 | 3 | 64.00 | 64.00 | 67.00 |
| Greece | 7 | 63.00 | 3 | 52.00 | 52.00 | 58.00 |
| Spain | 7 | 39.00 | 3 | 42.00 | 42.00 | 45.00 |
| Germany | 6 | 67.00 | 1 | 78.00 | 78.00 | 81.00 |
| Sweden | 6 | 55.00 | 3 | 78.00 | 78.00 | 79.00 |
| Finland | 5 | 65.00 | 3 | 45.00 | 45.00 | 50.00 |
| Luxembourg | 4 | 44.00 | - | - | - | - |
| Bermuda | 3 | 50.00 | - | - | - | - |
| Denmark | 3 | 61.00 | 2 | 43.00 | 41.00 | 40.00 |
| Ireland | 3 | 65.00 | 2 | 43.00 | 43.00 | 45.00 |
| Italy | 3 | 60.00 | 1 | 44.00 | 44.00 | 43.00 |
| Kenya | 3 | 77.00 | 1 | 53.00 | 53.00 | 63.00 |

(continued)

Appendix D. (cont.)

| Country | Disclosure | | Value relevance | | | |
|---|---|---|---|---|---|---|
| | Number of firms | Disclosure index | Number of firms | Disclosure index | | |
| | | 2011 | | 2011 | 2012 | 2013 |
| Netherlands | 3 | 57.00 | 1 | 74.00 | 74.00 | 82.00 |
| Portugal | 3 | 59.00 | 2 | 50.00 | 50.00 | 50.00 |
| Belgium | 2 | 50.00 | 1 | 82.00 | 82.00 | 87.00 |
| Lithuania | 2 | 92.00 | 1 | 76.00 | 81.00 | 84.00 |
| Peru | 2 | 58.00 | 1 | 77.00 | 77.00 | 83.00 |
| Ukraine | 2 | 50.00 | 1 | 53.00 | 53.00 | 53.00 |
| Cyprus | 1 | 27.00 | 1 | 36.00 | 36.00 | 35.00 |
| Oman | 2 | 14.00 | - | - | - | - |
| Russian Federation | 2 | 44.00 | - | - | - | - |
| Austria | 1 | 38.00 | - | - | - | - |
| Cayman islands | 1 | 50.00 | - | - | - | - |
| Croatia | 1 | 47.00 | - | - | - | - |
| Egypt | 1 | 63.00 | - | - | - | - |
| Faroe Islands | 1 | 44.00 | - | - | - | - |
| Kuwait | 1 | 00.00 | - | - | - | - |
| Latvia | 1 | 07.00 | - | - | - | - |
| Mauritius | 1 | 76.00 | - | - | - | - |
| United Arab Emirates | 1 | 71.00 | - | - | - | - |
| Papua New Guinea | - | - | 1 | 72.00 | 72.00 | 69.00 |
| Total | 270 | | 132 | | | |

*Appendix E.* Pearson's correlation

| Disclosure | INDEX | BIO | HELD | SIZE | INT | ROE |
|---|---|---|---|---|---|---|
| INDEX | | | | | | |
| BIO | 0.428*** | | | | | |
| HELD | 0.118 | −0.009 | | | | |
| SIZE | 0.001 | −0.121* | 0.230*** | | | |
| INT | 0.053 | 0.163** | −0.090 | 0.268*** | | |
| ROE | 0.086 | 0.091 | −0.006 | 0.231*** | 0.036 | |

| Measurement | BIO | SIZE | IFRS | GROWTH | LEV | QUALITY |
|---|---|---|---|---|---|---|
| BIO | | | | | | |
| SIZE | −0.113** | | | | | |
| IFRS | 0.022 | 0.020 | | | | |
| GROWTH | −0.187*** | 0.070 | 0.025 | | | |
| LEV | −0.055 | 0.166*** | −0.097* | 0.066 | | |
| QUALITY | 0.233*** | −0.014 | 0.106* | −0.318*** | −0.008 | |

| Value Relevance | MV | BV | BV-BA | BA | E | SIZE |
|---|---|---|---|---|---|---|
| MV | | | | | | |
| BV | 0.887*** | | | | | |
| BV-BA | 0.812*** | 0.949*** | | | | |
| BA | 0.757*** | 0.789*** | 0.554*** | | | |
| E | 0.787*** | 0.733*** | 0.642*** | 0.682*** | | |
| SIZE | 0.304*** | 0.245*** | 0.297*** | 0.067 | 0.18*** | |

Statistical significance at: *** 1% level; ** 5% level; * 10% level

*Appendix F.* OLS regression model

| Equation: | (2) | | (3) | |
|---|---|---|---|---|
| Selection: | 1 269 | | 1 269 | |
| Included: | 187 | | 180 | |
| Dependent variable: | INDEX | | INDEX | |
| *Variable* | *coef.* | *t-stat.* | *t-stat.* | *coef.* |
| Constant | 9.117 | 0.632 | 11.943 | 0.787 |
| BIO | 0.704 | 4.161*** | 0.781 | 4.202*** |
| HELD | 0.118 | 2.212** | 0.114 | 2.196** |
| SIZE | 1.873 | 1.881* | 1.646 | 1.611* |
| AUDIT | 0.989 | 0.271 | −1.116 | −0.286 |
| INT | −0.036 | −0.992 | −0.026 | −0.693 |
| STOCK | −4.523 | −1.192 | −4.833 | −1.221 |
| ROE | 0.017 | 0.187 | 0.005 | 0.049 |
| SECTOR1=1 | 13.462 | 2.920*** | 10.738 | 2.456** |
| SECTOR2=1 | 11.249 | 2.591** | 10.112 | 2.482** |
| LEGAL | 5.451 | 1.821* | | |
| CLUSTER1=1 | | | 6.679 | 1.681* |
| CLUSTER2=1 | | | 1.956 | 0.514 |
| Adjusted R-squared | 0.215 | | 0.235 | |
| F-statistic | 6.089*** | | 5.985*** | |

Statistical significance at: *** 1% level; ** 5% level; * 10% level

| Equation: | (4) | | (5) | | (6) | |
|---|---|---|---|---|---|---|
| Selection: 1 269 | *coef.* | *t-stat.* | *coef.* | *t-stat.* | *coef.* | *t-stat.* |
| AUD08 | −0.111 | −2.051** | | | | |
| ENF08 | | | −0.064 | −1.077 | | |
| AUD08_ENF08 | | | | | −0.104 | −1.738* |
| Adjusted R-squared | | 0.329 | | 0.315 | | 0.324 |
| F-statistic | | 8.858*** | | 8.374*** | | 8.663*** |

Statistical significance at: *** 1% level; ** 5% level; * 10% level

*Appendix G.* Chi-squared test between biological assets and measurement practice

| Count | Consumable | | | | Bearer | | | | Total |
|---|---|---|---|---|---|---|---|---|---|
| | Crops | Live | Other consumable | Sub total | Dairy | Vines | Other bearer | Sub total | |
| Historical cost | 8 | 32 | 10 | 50 | 7 | 33 | 14 | 54 | 104 |
| Fair value | 57 | 45 | 19 | 121 | 10 | 54 | 35 | 99 | 220 |
| Total | **65** | **77** | **29** | **171** | **17** | **87** | **49** | **153** | **324** |

| Likelihood ratio | Df | Value | Prob |
|---|---|---|---|
| All | 5 | 19.145 | 0.002 |
| Consumable | 2 | 16.272 | 0.001 |
| Bearer | 2 | 1.517 | 0.469 |

| Measures of association | Phi coefficient | Cramer's V | Contingency coefficient |
|---|---|---|---|
| All | 0.230 | 0.230 | 0.225 |
| Consumable | 0.297 | 0.297 | 0.284 |
| Bearer | 0.099 | 0.099 | 0.098 |

*Appendix H.* Number of firms by country with the related measurement practice

| Nation | Historical cost | Fair value | Total |
|---|---|---|---|
| Australia | 1 | 20 | 21 |
| Belgium | - | 2 | 2 |
| Brazil | 7 | 22 | 29 |
| Canada | - | 6 | 6 |
| Cayman Islands | - | 1 | 1 |
| Chile | 11 | 15 | 26 |
| China | 54 | 13 | 67 |
| Denmark | - | 3 | 3 |
| Finland | - | 4 | 4 |
| France | 3 | 4 | 7 |
| Germany | 1 | 3 | 4 |
| Greece | - | 7 | 7 |
| Hong Kong | 1 | 25 | 26 |
| Ireland | - | 2 | 2 |
| Italy | 2 | – | 2 |
| Kenya | - | 2 | 2 |
| Korea (South) | 14 | 4 | 18 |
| Kuwait | 1 | – | 1 |
| Lithuania | - | 1 | 1 |
| Luxembourg | - | 5 | 5 |
| Netherlands | - | 3 | 3 |
| New Zealand | - | 10 | 10 |
| Norway | - | 5 | 5 |
| Oman | 1 | 1 | 2 |
| Peru | - | 2 | 2 |
| Philippines | 4 | 5 | 9 |
| Poland | - | 1 | 1 |
| Portugal | 1 | 2 | 3 |
| South Africa | - | 18 | 18 |
| Spain | 3 | 4 | 7 |
| Sweden | - | 9 | 9 |
| United Arab Emirates | - | 2 | 2 |
| United Kingdom | - | 19 | 19 |
| Total | **104** | **220** | **324** |

*Appendix I.* Logit regression model

| Equation: | (7) | | | (8) | | |
|---|---|---|---|---|---|---|
| Selection: | 1 324 | | | 1 324 | | |
| Included observations: | 319 after adjustments | | | 319 after adjustments | | |
| Dependent variable: | FAIR | | | FAIR | | |
| Standard errors & covariance: | QML (Huber/White) | | | QML (Huber/White) | | |
| | | | | | | |
| Variable | odds ratio | coefficient | z-statistic | odds ratio | coefficient | z-statistic |
| Constant | 0.003 | -5.875 | -4.027*** | 0.003 | -5.868 | -4.067*** |
| BIO | 1.082 | 0.079 | 2.832*** | 1.083 | 0.079 | 2.842*** |
| SIZE | 1.698 | 0.530 | 2.608*** | 1.739 | 0.553 | 2.716*** |
| STOCK | 15.370 | 2.732 | 2.968*** | 15.792 | 2.759 | 2.961*** |
| IFRS | 19.735 | 2.982 | 3.833*** | 15.577 | 2.746 | 3.460*** |
| GROWTH | 0.805 | -0.217 | -1.938* | 0.801 | -0.222 | -2.074** |
| LEV | 1.091 | 0.087 | 0.903 | 1.087 | 0.083 | 0.851 |
| SECTOR1+SECTOR2=1 | 1.914 | 0.649 | 1.767* | | | |
| IFRS*(SECTOR1+SECTOR2=1) | | | | 3.226 | 1.171 | 2.432** |
| QUALITY | 3.911 | 1.364 | 6.366*** | 3.924 | 1.367 | 6.338*** |
| McFadden R-squared | | 0.374 | | | 0.378 | |
| Log likelihood | | -126.081 | | | -125.277 | |
| Restr. log likelihood | | -201.392 | | | -201.392 | |
| LR statistic | | 150.622*** | | | 152.230*** | |
| Obs with Dep=0 | | 104 | | | 104 | |
| Obs with Dep=1 | | 215 | | | 215 | |
| Total obs | | 319 | | | 319 | |

Statistical significance at: *** 1% level; ** 5% level; * 10% level

*Appendix J.* Expectation-prediction evaluation for binary specification

| Estimated equation | Dep = 0 | Dep = 1 | Total |
|---|---|---|---|
| P(Dep=1)<=C | 75 | 22 | **97** |
| P(Dep=1)>C | 29 | 193 | **222** |
| Total | 104 | 215 | **319** |
| Correct | 75 | 193 | **268** |
| % Correct | 72.12 | 89.77 | **84.01** |
| % Incorrect | 27.88 | 10.23 | **15.99** |

*Appendix K.* Goodness-of-fit evaluation for binary specification

| Statistic | (7) | (8) |
|---|---|---|
| Hosmer–Lemeshow | 13.943 | 16.066 |
| Prob.Chi-Sq (8) | 0.083 | 0.041 |
| Andrews | 35.464 | 37.008 |
| Prob.Chi-Sq (10) | 0.000 | 0.000 |

*Appendix L.* Robustness test – sectors: agriculture versus manufacturing

| Equation: | (7) | | (8) | |
|---|---|---|---|---|
| Variable | *odds ratio* | *odds ratio* | *odds ratio* | *odds ratio* |
| Constant | 0.003*** | 0.005*** | 0.003*** | 0.003*** |
| BIO | 1.082*** | 1.085*** | 1.083*** | 1.087*** |
| SIZE | 1.699*** | 1.644** | 1.739*** | 1.668** |
| STOCK | 15.364*** | 15.211*** | 15.792*** | 15.532*** |
| IFRS | 19.727*** | 22.669*** | 15.577*** | 40.476*** |
| GROWTH | 0.805* | 0.811* | 0.801** | 0.812* |
| LEV | 1.091 | 1.100 | 1.087 | 1.090 |
| SECTOR1=1 | 1.914* | | | |
| SECTOR2=1 | | 0.480** | | |
| IFRS*SECTOR1=1 | | | 3.226** | |
| IFRS*SECTOR2=1 | | | | 0.363** |
| QUALITY | 3.912*** | 3.827*** | 3.924*** | 3.868*** |
| McFadden R-squared | 0.374 | 0.379 | 0.378 | 0.379 |
| Log likelihood | −126.081 | −124.976 | −125.277 | −125.142 |
| Restr. log likelihood | −201.392 | −201.392 | −201.392 | −201.392 |
| LR statistic | 150.622*** | 152.832*** | 152.230*** | 152.500*** |
| Obs with Dep=0 | 104 | 104 | 104 | 104 |
| Obs with Dep=1 | 215 | 215 | 215 | 215 |
| Total obs | 319 | 319 | 319 | 319 |

Statistical significance at: *** 1% level; ** 5% level; * 10% level

Appendix M. Robustness test – sectors: agriculture versus manufacturing (details)

| Equation: (6) | Agriculture | | Manufacturing | | |
| --- | --- | --- | --- | --- | --- |
| | Crops | Livestock and Animal Specialties | Paper and Allied Products | Food and Kindred Products | Beverages |
| Variable | odds ratio | odds ratio | odds ratio | odds ratio | odds ratio |
| Constant | 0.003*** | 0.003*** | 0.007*** | 0.006*** | 0.006*** |
| BIO | 1.083*** | 1.084*** | 1.082*** | 1.084*** | 1.089*** |
| SIZE | 1.693*** | 1.676** | 1.575** | 1.580** | 1.569** |
| STOCK | 15.292*** | 15.808*** | 15.684*** | 15.172*** | 16.496*** |
| IFRS | 19.792*** | 20.039*** | 23.314*** | 24.909*** | 25.647*** |
| GROWTH | 0.803** | 0.805** | 0.823* | 0.822** | 0.829* |
| LEV | 1.091 | 1.093 | 1.088 | 1.101 | 1.078 |
| subSECTOR1.01=1 | 1.702 | | | | |
| subSECTOR1.02=1 | | 1.239 | | | |
| subSECTOR1.01oth=1 | 2.003** | | | | |
| subSECTOR1.02oth=1 | | 2.311* | | | |
| subSECTOR2.26=1 | | | 0.912 | | |
| subSECTOR2.20=1 | | | | 0.367*** | |
| subSECTOR2.208=1 | | | | | 0.139*** |
| subSECTOR2.26oth=1 | | | 0.441** | | |
| subSECTOR2.20oth=1 | | | | 0.704 | |
| subSECTOR2.208oth=1 | | | | | 0.654 |
| QUALITY | 3.911*** | 3.854*** | 3.853*** | 3.904*** | 4.510*** |

| | | | | | |
|---|---|---|---|---|---|
| McFadden R-squared | 0.374 | 0.376 | 0.382 | 0.385 | 0.400 |
| Log likelihood | -126.057 | -125.709 | -124.335 | -123.788 | -120.817 |
| Restr. log likelihood | -201.392 | -201.392 | -201.392 | -201.392 | -201.392 |
| LR statistic | 150.670*** | 151.366*** | 154.115*** | 155.208*** | 161.150*** |
| Obs with Dep=0 | 104 | 104 | 104 | 104 | 104 |
| Obs with Dep=1 | 215 | 215 | 215 | 215 | 215 |
| Total obs | 319 | 319 | 319 | 319 | 319 |

SubSECTOR1.01 Agricultural Production – Crops
SubSECTOR1.02 Agricultural Production – Livestock and Animal Specialties
SubSECTOR2.26 Paper and Allied Products
SubSECTOR2.20 Food and Kindred Products
SubSECTOR2.208 Beverages
Statistical significance at: *** 1% level; ** 5% level; * 10% level

*Appendix N.* Panel fixed effects regression model

| Equation: | (9) | | (10) | | (11) | |
|---|---|---|---|---|---|---|
| Selection: | 2011 2013 | | 2011 2013 | | 2011 2013 | |
| Included panel observ: | 389 | | 389 | | 389 | |
| Dependent variable: | MV | | MV | | MV | |
| Variable | *coef.* | *t-stat.* | *coef.* | *t-stat.* | *coef.* | *t-stat.* |
| Constant | -10.499 | -3.567*** | -11.774 | -4.792*** | -10.271 | -3.952*** |
| BV | 0.668 | 5.597*** | | | | |
| BV-BA | | | 0.596 | 4.894*** | 0.668 | 4.234*** |
| BA | | | 0.881 | 3.221*** | 0.507 | 1.700* |
| E | 2.608 | 2.415** | 2.406 | 2.266** | 2.432 | 2.567** |
| $Dindex_1$ | | | | | 1.212 | 1.418 |
| $Dindex_3$ | | | | | -0.622 | -1.232 |
| $Dindex_1$ x BA | | | | | 1.402 | 0.912 |
| $Dindex_3$ x BA | | | | | 0.797 | 3.088*** |
| Controls | | | | | | |
| SIZE | 1.963 | 3.752*** | 2.258 | 5.734*** | 1.863 | 4.636*** |
| SECTOR1+SECTOR2=1 | 1.136 | 1.281 | 0.711 | 0.849 | 0.881 | 1.031 |
| Adjusted R-squared | 0.835 | | 0.838 | | 0.858 | |
| F-statistic | 327.428*** | | 287.464*** | | 213.358*** | |

Statistical significance at: *** 1% level; ** 5% level; * 10% level

*Appendix O.* Bearer and consumable biological assets classification

*Panel A: Panel fixed effects regression results*

| Variables | Bearer | | Consumable | |
|---|---|---|---|---|
| | coef. | t-stat. | coef. | t-stat. |
| Constant | −20.759 | −3.957*** | −3.394 | −1.737* |
| BV-BA | 0.549 | 3.345*** | 0.821 | 8.612*** |
| BA | 0.649 | 1.943* | 1.148 | 3.247*** |
| E | 2.497 | 2.405** | 1.781 | 1.752* |
| $Dindex_1$ | 3.667 | 1.779* | −0.410 | −1.101 |
| $Dindex_3$ | −0.912 | −1.035 | −0.312 | −0.549 |
| $Dindex_1$ x BA | 4.180 | 1.327 | −1.239 | −1.376 |
| $Dindex_3$ x BA | 1.029 | 3.673*** | 0.040 | 0.117 |
| Controls | | | | |
| SIZE | 3.745 | 4.470*** | 0.689 | 2.001** |
| SECTOR1+SECTOR2=1 | 1.295 | 0.893 | −0.012 | −0.023 |
| N | 167 | | 222 | |
| Adjusted R-squared | 0.866 | | 0.878 | |
| F-statistic | 98.907*** | | 145.717*** | |

*Panel B: Chow test for equation (4.4) – all, bearer and consumable*

| Sum squared residuals | All | Bearer | Consumable |
|---|---|---|---|
| | 14077.14 | 9880.421 | 2285.219 |
| Number of parameters | 10 | | |
| Number of observations | 389 | 167 | 222 |
| F-statistic(10,369) | 5.798 | | |

Statistical significance at: *** 1% level; ** 5% level; * 10% level

*Appendix P.* Robustness test – market value six months after fiscal year-end

| Equation: | (9) | | (10) | | (11) | |
|---|---|---|---|---|---|---|
| Selection: | 2011 2013 | | 2011 2013 | | 2011 2013 | |
| Included panel observ.: | 386 | | 386 | | 386 | |
| Dependent variable: | $MV_{6m}$ | | $MV_{6m}$ | | $MV_{6m}$ | |
| *Variable* | *coef.* | *t-stat.* | *coef.* | *t-stat.* | *coef.* | *t-stat.* |
| Constant | −11.251 | −3.664*** | −12.263 | −4.806*** | −11.848 | −4.467*** |
| BV | 0.640 | 6.099*** | | | | |
| BV-BA | | | 0.584 | 4.962*** | 0.616 | 4.125*** |
| BA | | | 0.809 | 3.410*** | 0.623 | 1.947* |
| E | 2.453 | 2.714*** | 2.293 | 2.565** | 2.294 | 2.725*** |
| $Dindex_1$ | | | | | 1.401 | 1.632 |
| $Dindex_3$ | | | | | −0.341 | −0.687 |
| $Dindex_1$ x BA | | | | | 0.385 | 0.271 |
| $Dindex_3$ x BA | | | | | 0.429 | 1.558 |
| Controls | | | | | | |
| SIZE | 2.069 | 3.815*** | 2.303 | 5.570*** | 2.127 | 5.226*** |
| SECTOR1+SECTOR2=1 | 1.153 | 1.299 | 0.821 | 0.946 | 0.960 | 1.067 |
| Adjusted R-squared | 0.837 | | 0.839 | | 0.845 | |
| F-statistic | 329.571*** | | 286.921*** | | 191.682*** | |

$MV_{6m}$ – market value per share that equals the market price month close (6 months after the fiscal year-end).
Statistical significance at: *** 1% level; ** 5% level; * 10% level

*Appendix Q.* Robustness test – firms above first quartile of biological assets per share selection's distribution

| Equation: | (10) | | | (11) | | |
|---|---|---|---|---|---|---|
| Selection: | 2011 2013 | | | 2011 2013 | | |
| Included panel observ: | 289 | | | 289 | | |
| Dependent variable: | MV | | | MV | | |
| *Variable* | *coef.* | *t-stat.* | | *coef.* | *t-stat.* | |
| Constant | −11.689 | −3.565*** | | −9.566 | −3.007*** | |
| BV-BA$_{0.25}$ | 0.616 | 4.776*** | | 0.693 | 4.118*** | |
| BA$_{0.25}$ | 0.964 | 3.641*** | | 0.590 | 1.902* | |
| E | 1.909 | 2.020** | | 1.921 | 2.388** | |
| Dindex$_1$ | | | | 0.837 | 0.683 | |
| Dindex$_3$ | | | | −0.853 | −1.642 | |
| Dindex$_1$ x BA$_{0.25}$ | | | | 1.875 | 0.970 | |
| Dindex$_3$ x BA$_{0.25}$ | | | | 0.796 | 2.920*** | |
| Controls | | | | | | |
| SIZE | 2.268 | 4.701*** | | 1.806 | 3.890*** | |
| SECTOR1+SECTOR2=1 | 0.562 | 0.464 | | 0.561 | 0.488 | |
| Adjusted R-squared | 0.844 | | | 0.865 | | |
| F-statistic | 223.699*** | | | 168.363*** | | |

BA$_{0.25}$ – Biological assets (WS18277, WS18278 or WS18258) divided by common shares outstanding (WS05301) above first quartile of biological assets per share distribution.

Statistical significance at: *** 1% level; ** 5% level; * 10% level

# Annexes

*Annex A.* Leuz's (2010) cluster classification

| Cluster 1 | Cluster 2 | Cluster 3 | |
|---|---|---|---|
| Australia | Singapore | Austria | Japan | Argentina | Pakistan |
| Canada | South Africa | Belgium | Korea (South) | Brazil | Philippines |
| Hong Kong | United Kingdom | Chile | Netherlands | Colombia | Portugal |
| Ireland | United States | Denmark | Norway | Greece | Taiwan |
| Israel | | Finland | Spain | India | Thailand |
| Malaysia | | France | Sweden | Italy | |
| New Zealand | | Germany | Switzerland | Mexico | |

Cluster membership using regulatory and reporting practice variables

*Annex B.* Brown *et al.* (2014) classification

| | Audit | Enforce | Total |
|---|---|---|---|
| *Countries that adopted IFRS in 2005* | | | |
| Australia | 30 | 22 | **52** |
| Austria | 19 | 8 | **27** |
| Belgium | 22 | 22 | **44** |
| Croatia | 14 | 8 | **22** |
| Czech Republic | 11 | 8 | **19** |
| Denmark | 27 | 22 | **49** |
| Finland | 20 | 12 | **32** |
| France | 29 | 16 | **45** |
| Germany | 23 | 21 | **44** |
| Greece | 17 | 9 | **26** |
| Hong Kong | 30 | 22 | **52** |
| Hungary | 6 | 12 | **18** |
| Ireland | 29 | 12 | **41** |
| Italy | 27 | 19 | **46** |
| Netherlands | 24 | 19 | **43** |
| Norway | 25 | 22 | **47** |
| Poland | 19 | 9 | **28** |
| Portugal | 17 | 12 | **29** |
| Romania | 6 | 9 | **15** |
| Slovenia | 11 | 8 | **19** |
| South Africa | 19 | 10 | **29** |
| Singapore | 20 | 12 | **32** |
| Spain | 26 | 16 | **42** |
| Sweden | 25 | 9 | **34** |
| Switzerland | 27 | 22 | **49** |
| Ukraine | 4 | 2 | **6** |
| United Kingdom | 32 | 22 | **54** |
| *Countries that did not adopt IFRS in 2005* | | | |
| Argentina | 9 | 2 | **11** |
| Brazil | 15 | 8 | **23** |
| Canada | 32 | 22 | **54** |
| Chile | 4 | 5 | **9** |
| China | 21 | 16 | **37** |
| Egypt | 10 | 4 | **14** |
| India | 15 | 6 | **21** |
| Indonesia | 8 | 6 | **14** |
| Israel | 24 | 24 | **48** |
| Japan | 26 | 8 | **34** |
| Jordan | 6 | 5 | **11** |
| Korea (South) | 18 | 10 | **28** |
| Malaysia | 21 | 19 | **40** |
| Mexico | 12 | 13 | **25** |
| Morocco | 9 | 2 | **11** |

(*continued*)

|  | Audit | Enforce | Total |
|---|---|---|---|
| New Zealand | 24 | 19 | **43** |
| Pakistan | 10 | 8 | **18** |
| Peru | 11 | 5 | **16** |
| Philippines | 11 | 16 | **27** |
| Russia | 22 | 6 | **28** |
| Taiwan | 10 | 8 | **18** |
| Thailand | 11 | 12 | **23** |
| Turkey | 11 | 9 | **20** |
| United States | 32 | 24 | **56** |

Comparison of audit and enforcement scores by country for 2008

# Index

Bold page numbers indicate tables.

Printed in the United States
by Baker & Taylor Publisher Services